Copyright © Victoria Green, 2023

All rights reserved. This book or parts thereof may not be reproduced in any form, stored in any retrieval system, or transmitted in any form by any mean — electronic, mechanical, photocopy, recording, or otherwise — without prior written permission of the publisher, except by a reviewer who may quote brief passages in a review.

Disclaimer: the author is not responsible for the outcome of any recipe you try from the book. You may not achieve desired results due to variations in elements such as ingredients, cooking temperatures, typos, errors, omissions, or individual cooking ability. You should always use your best judgment when cooking with raw ingredients such as eggs, chicken, or seafood and seek expert advice before beginning if you are unsure. Please review all ingredients prior to trying a recipe in order to be fully aware of the presence of substances which might cause an adverse reaction in some consumers.

The author is not a healthcare practitioner. All information represented in the book is purely for informational and educational purposes. Information is not intended to treat, cure or prevent any disease. Statements within this book have not been approved by the FDA. The writer or publisher of this book are not responsible for any adverse reactions, effects, or consequences resulting from the use of any recipes or suggestions herein.

Table of Contents

Introduction 8
Breakfast 9
    Ham Frittata 9
    Vanilla Pancakes 9
    Sausage Frittata 10
    Breakfast Meat Casserole 10
    Egg Casserole 11
    Slow Cooker Veggie Egg Bake 11
    Bacon Omelette 12
    Cheesy Turmeric Eggs 12
    Cauliflower Hash Brown 12
    Egg Quiche 13
    Breakfast Ground Beef Casserole 13
    Salmon and Avocado Breakfast Bake 14
    Broccoli Muffins 14
    Eggs with Greens 15
    Breakfast Bowl 15
    Keto Egg Muffins 15
    Brussel Sprouts Eggs 16
    Breakfast Meat Bowl 16
    Egg Bars 16
    Breakfast Turkey Roll 17
    Breakfast Bacon and Eggs 17
    Keto Porridge 18
    Mushroom Omelette 18
    Western Omelette 18
    Slow Cooker Sausages 19
    Coconut Porridge 19
    Salmon Cutlets 20
    Bacon Beef Casserole 20
    Breakfast Tender Chicken Strips 21
    Chicken Muffins 21
    Vanilla Pancakes 21
    Veggie Turkey Smash 22
    Paprika Shrimp 22
    Breakfast Pizza 22
    Breakfast Sweet Pepper Hash 23
    Pork Breakfast Sausages 23
    Chicken Bites 23
    Avocado Boats 24
    Cabbage Rolls 24
    Collard Greens 25
    Breakfast Pie 25

Cod Bites	26
Moroccan Meatballs	26
Breakfast Shredded Pork	27
Bacon Pecan Bok Choy	27
Chia Seeds Pudding	27
Prosciutto Chicken Nuggets	28
Avocado Tuna Balls	28
Basil Meatballs	28
Kale Frittata	29
Main Dishes	30
Keto Lasagna	30
Butter Chicken	30
Tuscan Chicken	31
Corned Beef	31
Sardine Pate	32
Spare Ribs	32
Pork Shoulder	32
Lamb Chops	33
Rosemary Leg of Lamb	33
Creamy Chicken Thighs	34
Peppered Steak	34
Rabbit Stew	34
Duck Breast	35
Jerk Chicken	35
Balsamic Beef	36
Beef Curry	36
Keto Chili	37
Ground Pork Bowl	37
Chili Verde	38
Marinated Greek Style Pork	38
Shredded Chicken	38
Keto Beef Ribs	39
Bacon Meatloaf	39
Keto Pork Tenderloin	39
Lamb Stew	40
Delicious Turmeric Beef Stew	40
Asian Chopped Beef	40
Spicy Bacon Strips	41
Paprika Pork Sausages	41
Chicken Stew	41
Pulled Pork Salad	42
Garlic Pork Belly	42
Sesame Seed Shrimp	42
Cod Fillet in Coconut Flakes	43

Chicken Liver Pate	43
Garlic Duck Breast	43
Thyme Lamb Chops	44
Autumn Pork Stew	44
Handmade Sausage Stew	44
Marinated Beef Tenderloin	45
Chicken Liver Sauté	45
Chicken in Bacon	46
Whole Chicken	46
Duck Rolls	46
Keto Adobo Chicken	47
Cayenne Pepper Drumsticks	47
Keto BBQ Chicken Wings	47
Prawn Stew	48
Pork-Jalapeno Bowl	48
Chicken Marsala	48
Side Dishes	49
Zucchini Pasta	49
Chinese Broccoli	49
Slow Cooker Spaghetti Squash	49
Mushroom Stew	50
Cabbage Steaks	50
Mashed Cauliflower	50
Bacon Wrapped Cauliflower	51
Cauliflower Casserole	51
Cauliflower Rice	51
Curry Cauliflower	52
Garlic Cauliflower Steaks	52
Zucchini Gratin	52
Eggplant Gratin	53
Moroccan Eggplant Mash	53
Sautéed Bell Peppers	54
Garlic Artichoke	54
Broccoli Stew	54
Spiced Fennel Slices	55
Okra Stew	55
Sesame Snow Peas	55
Coconut Kale	56
Tomato Gratin with Bell Pepper	56
Spicy Mushrooms	56
Cumin Green Beans	57
Zucchini Fettuccine	57
Vegetable Stew	57
Brussel Sprouts with Parmesan	58

Garlic Peppers	58
Tender Green Cabbage	58
Curled Rutabaga	59
Layered Mushrooms	59
Rutabaga Wedges	59
Thai Cabbage	60
Eggplant Hash	60
Creamy Eggplant Salad	60
Slow Cooker Broccoli Rabe	61
Soft Keto Kale Salad	61
Keto Leeks	61
Green Bean and Avocado Salad	62
Red Cabbage Slices	62
Cauliflower Puree with Parmesan	62
Cauliflower Croquettes	63
Grated Zucchini with Cheese	63
Cheesy Spaghetti Squash	63
Pesto Spaghetti Squash	64
Zucchini Slices with Mozzarella	64
Kale Mash with Blue Cheese	64
Black Soybeans	65
Marinated Fennel Bulb	65
Pumpkin Cubes	65
Snacks and Appetizers	66
Wrapped Avocado Sticks	66
Deviled Eggs	66
Turkey Meatballs	66
Chicken and Cauliflower Pizza	67
Cauliflower Bites	67
Wrapped Prawns in Bacon	67
Buffalo Chicken Wings	68
Eggplant Fries	68
Parmesan Green Beans	68
Zucchini Fries	69
Cauliflower Fritters	69
Zucchini Latkes	69
Zucchini Tots with Cheese	70
Spicy & Salty Keto Nuts	70
Jalapeno Fritters	70
Onion Rings	71
Keto Tortillas with Cheese	71
Sweet and Spicy Chicken Wings	71
Ground Chicken Pepper Meatballs	72
Pork Nuggets	72

Meat Balls with Mozzarella	72
Pulled Pork	73
Crunchy Bacon	73
Seasoned Mini Meatballs	73
Mini Chicken Meatballs	74
Spinach Rolls	74
Pork Belly Bites	74
Sweet Brussel Sprouts	75
Mushroom Skewers	75
Tilapia Bites	75
Stuffed Mushrooms	76
Asian Pork with Keto Tortillas	76
Caprese Meatballs	76
Chicken Tenders	77
Garlic Chicken Wings	77
Broccoli Balls	77
White Queso Dip	78
Keto Bread Sticks	78
Cheesy Zucchini Crisps	78
Keto Crackers	79
Chia Crackers	79
Crab Dip with Mushrooms	79
Artichoke Hummus	80
Cauliflower Bread	80
Bacon Wrapped Duck Roll	80
Eggplant Bacon Fries	81
Mushroom Stuffed Meatballs	81
Bacon Pepper Quiche	81
Mini Muffins	82
Eggplant Rolls with Meat	82
Desserts	83
Keto Chocolate Bars	83
Keto Cobbler	83
Soft Bacon Cookies	84
Keto Brownies	84
Keto Peanut Butter Cookies	84
Mint Pudding	85
Keto Chip Cookies	85
Coconut Bars	85
Spoon Cake	86
Sweet Bacon Slices	86
Pound Cake	86
Sweet Sesame Buns	87
Almond Cookies	87

Avocado Muffins	87
Walnut Balls	88
Rhubarb Crumble	88
Blueberry Pie	88
Sesame Cookies	89
Keto Soufflé	89
Sweet Zucchini Muffins	89
Chocolate Mousse	90
Keto Truffles	90
Coconut Bars	90
Candied Almonds	91
Vanilla Cream	91
Snowball Cookies	91
Dessert Pancakes	92
Cinnamon Cup Cake	92
Pudding Cake	92
Keto Fudge	93
Kombucha Cake	93
Gingerbread Cookies	93
Chewy Seed and Nut Bars	94
Red Velvet Cupcakes	94
Keto Cheesecake	94
Lavender Cookies	95
Mini Pumpkin Cakes	95
Walnut Muffins	96
Vanilla Rolls	96
Cinnamon Swirls	96
Lava Cake	97
Keto Sweet Bread	97
Avocado Bars	97
Raspberry Tart	98
Rhubarb Bars	98
Pecan Cookies	98
Flax Seeds Balls	99
Sunflower Seeds Cookies	99
Tender Lime Cake	99
Keto Almond Scones	100
Conclusion	**101**
Recipe Index	**102**

Introduction

A slow cooker is one of the most useful kitchen appliance that gives you the ability to cook ordinary food sin better, easier and healthier way. If you have never heard of a slow cooker before, perhaps you are familiar with a crock pot. If so, they are one and the same! Slow cookers and crock pots are both kitchen appliances that cook food for hours over a very low temperature, helping combine flavors, break down proteins and make foods tender and moist.

There are many types of the slow cookers, from cheap to very expensive, fancy to basic, so it is easy to find one for your budget and family. Of course, a slow cooker is a piece of electrical equipment so it should always be used carefully. No matter what kind of slow cooker you purchase, remember to always read the manual before you begin!

Cooking foods slowly over very low heat can save all the useful minerals and vitamins in foods that usually "die" at the high temperatures of other cooking methods. The golden rule of the slow cooker is "low is better".

Slow cookers are used all over the world not only because of its economical features but also because of how easy it is to use. The kitchen appliance can basically cook a whole meal all by itself without any help. All you have to do is put all the ingredients in the machine, set the mode and time and wait until the meal is cooked. It really is that easy! You can walk away and come back hours later to a perfectly prepared meal thanks to this appliance.

The food also can be cooked with just a small amount of fat or even with none at all. The juice that is extracted from the ingredients is enough to cook the food in making fats and oils unnecessary. This may sound ideal if you are following a keto diet. With no fats or oils allowed on the Keto diet plan, you are in luck as the slow cooker will work great for you as well. There are plenty of recipes that you can make that will adhere to your dietary requirements and taste amazing thanks to the low and slow method of cooking.

As you can see, the slow cooker is one of the best kitchen appliance around if you want to cook healthy, nutritious food that doesn't take much effort or time. This book will help you to cook the most delicious keto meals for you and your family. Now you don't need to stress about what to cook for breakfast, dinner, or lunch, you have plenty of options right here! Also, you will find tasty and easy snacks and appetizers here as well! Follow the recipes strictly or add your own fresh ideas- everything in this book will come out great! Always remember that there is only one true golden secret to the perfect meal – always cook with love!

Breakfast

Ham Frittata
Prep time: 10 minutes | Cooking time: 3 hours | Servings: 4

Ingredients:
- 4 eggs
- 10 oz ham, chopped
- 1 teaspoon butter
- 1 tablespoon dried dill
- 1 tablespoon dried parsley
- ¼ teaspoon salt
- ¾ cup almond milk, unsweetened

Directions:
Whisk the eggs in a mixing bowl with a hand whisker. Add dried dill, chopped ham, dried parsley, salt, and almond milk. Whisk the mixture well. Add the butter to the slow cooker. Add egg mixture and close the lid. Cook the frittata for 3 hours on Low. Serve the cooked meal immediately!

Nutrition: calories 283, fat 22.2, fiber 2.1, carbs 5, protein 18.

Vanilla Pancakes
Prep time: 10 minutes | Cooking time: 2 hours | Servings: 6

Ingredients:
- 1 cup almond flour
- ¼ cup coconut flour
- 1 teaspoon stevia extract
- 4 eggs, beaten
- ½ cup almond milk
- 4 tablespoons water
- 1 teaspoon olive oil
- 1 teaspoon vanilla extract

Directions:
Mix together the almond flour and coconut flour. Add stevia extract and beaten eggs and stir well. Add almond milk and water and blend. Add the vanilla extract and olive oil and mix until smooth. Pour the pancake batter into the slow cooker and cover. Cook the pancake for 2 hours on High. Let the cooked pancake cool a little.

Nutrition: calories 143, fat 11.3, fiber 2.9, carbs 5.8, protein 5.8

Sausage Frittata

Prep time: 10 minutes | Cooking time: 3 hours | Servings: 6

Ingredients:
- 6 oz sausages, chopped
- 6 eggs, beaten
- ¾ cup almond milk
- 1 teaspoon butter, melted
- 1 tablespoon dried parsley
- ½ teaspoon salt
- 1 oz Parmesan, grated

Directions:
Whisk the eggs and combine them with the chopped sausages. Add almond milk and dried parsley. Add the salt, grated cheese, and melted butter. Stir and pour into the slow cooker. Close the lid and cook the meal for 3 hours on Low.

Nutrition: calories 249, fat 21.2, fiber 0.7, carbs 2.2, protein 13.3

Breakfast Meat Casserole

Prep time: 15 minutes | Cooking time: 7 hours | Servings: 4

Ingredients:
- 5 oz ground chicken
- 3 oz ground pork
- 1 teaspoon salt
- 3 oz Parmesan, grated
- 1 garlic clove, chopped
- 1 teaspoon dried oregano
- ½ teaspoon turmeric
- 1 teaspoon paprika
- 1 onion, chopped
- 1 tablespoon olive oil
- ¾ teaspoon thyme

Directions:
Spray the olive oil inside the slow cooker. Mix up together the ground pork, chopped garlic, dried oregano, turmeric, paprika, and thyme. Stir the mixture well. Place the meat in the slow cooker in one flat layer. Cover the ground pork layer with the chopped onion and grated cheese. Close the lid and cook the casserole for 7 hours on Low. Serve it warm!

Nutrition: calories 212, fat 11.6, fiber 1.1, carbs 4.4, protein 23.2

Egg Casserole

Prep time: 10 minutes | Cooking time: 2 hours | Servings: 4

Ingredients:
- 1 tomato, sliced
- 3 eggs
- 5 oz asparagus, chopped
- 4 oz Parmesan, chopped
- 1 oz fresh dill, chopped
- 1 teaspoon olive oil
- ¾ teaspoon salt
- 1 teaspoon paprika

Directions:

Mix up together olive oil, salt, paprika, chopped asparagus, and fresh dill. Place the mixture in the slow cooker. Add a layer of the sliced tomato. Beat the eggs and pour over the tomatoes then close the lid. Cook the casserole for 2 hours on High or until the eggs are solid.

Nutrition: calories 178, fat 11, fiber 2.1, carbs 7.5, protein 15.7

Slow Cooker Veggie Egg Bake

Prep time: 10 minutes | Cooking time: 4 hours | Servings: 2

Ingredients:
- 3 oz cauliflower, chopped
- 3 oz celery stalk, chopped
- 1 tablespoon butter
- 1 bell pepper, chopped
- 1 teaspoon paprika
- ½ teaspoon cayenne pepper
- ¾ teaspoon salt
- 2 eggs

Directions:

Mix together the chopped celery stalk, cauliflower, bell pepper, paprika, and cayenne pepper. Transfer the mix to the slow cooker. Add the butter. Beat the eggs in a separate bowl. Pour the whisked eggs into the slow cooker and stir gently. Close the lid and cook the meal for 4 hours on Low.

Nutrition: calories 155, fat 10.6, fiber 3.1, carbs 9.2, protein 7.5

Bacon Omelette

Prep time: 15 minutes | Cooking time: 3 hours | Servings: 4

Ingredients:
- 3 eggs, beaten
- ¼ cup almond milk
- ¼ teaspoon salt
- ¼ teaspoon ground black pepper
- 5 oz bacon, chopped
- 1 tablespoon butter

Directions:
Place the butter in the slow cooker. Add chopped bacon and sprinkle with the ground black pepper. Whisk together the eggs, almond milk, and salt in a separate bowl. Pour the egg mixture into the slow cooker and close the lid. Cook the omelet for 3 hours on High. the meal immediately!

Nutrition: calories 299, fat 24.6, fiber 0.4, carbs 1.7, protein 17.7

Cheesy Turmeric Eggs

Prep time: 10 minutes | Cooking time: 1 hour 30 minutes | Servings: 4

Ingredients:
- 4 eggs, beaten
- ¾ teaspoon turmeric
- 1 tablespoon butter, melted
- 3 tablespoons almond milk, unsweetened
- 2 oz Parmesan, grated

Directions:
Whisk the eggs and with the turmeric, butter, and almond milk. Pour the mix into the slow cooker. Cook the eggs for 1 hours on High. Scramble the eggs with a spatula and sprinkle with the grated cheese. Cook the omelet for 30 minutes more on Low.

Nutrition: calories 161, fat 13, fiber 0.3, carbs 5, protein 10.4

Cauliflower Hash Brown

Prep time: 15 minutes | Cooking time: 5 hours | Servings: 5

Ingredients:
- 10 oz cauliflower, chopped
- 2 tablespoons butter
- 1 garlic clove, chopped
- 2 eggs, beaten
- 1 teaspoon ground black pepper
- 3 oz Parmesan, grated

Directions:
Place the butter and cauliflower in the slow cooker. Add garlic clove and ground black pepper. Add eggs and stir the mixture. Sprinkle the mixture with the grated cheese and close the lid. Cook the hash brown for 5 hours on Low. Then stir the hash brown and serve!

Nutrition: calories 137, fat 10.1, fiber 1.5, carbs 4.2, protein 8.9

Egg Quiche

Prep time: 15 minutes | Cooking time: 4 hours | Servings: 6

Ingredients:
- 1 cup almond flour
- ¼ cup almond milk
- ½ teaspoon salt
- 4 eggs, beaten
- 3 oz cauliflower, chopped
- 1 tomato, chopped
- 1 teaspoon paprika
- ¾ teaspoon ground black pepper
- ½ teaspoon turmeric
- 1 tablespoon butter
- 5 oz ground chicken

Directions:
Mix together the almond flour and almond milk until smooth. Add salt and beaten eggs. Whisk the mixture until smooth. Add chopped cauliflower, tomato, paprika, ground black pepper, turmeric, butter, and ground chicken. Mix well. Pour the quiche mixture into the slow cooker. Close the lid and cook the quiche for 4 hours on High. Let the cooked quiche cool slightly and serve!

Nutrition: calories 161, fat 11.4, fiber 1.4, carbs 3.4, protein 12.2

Breakfast Ground Beef Casserole

Prep time: 15 minutes | Cooking time: 7 hours | Servings: 4

Ingredients:
- 8 oz ground beef
- 1 zucchini, chopped
- 2 garlic cloves, chopped
- 3 oz mushrooms, chopped
- 2 tablespoons butter
- 1 teaspoon chili flakes
- 1 teaspoon ground black pepper
- ½ teaspoon salt

Directions:
Place the chopped zucchini in the slow cooker. Sprinkle the zucchini with the chopped garlic cloves. Add chili flakes and ground black pepper. Mix together salt and ground beef then add the butter and mix again. Transfer the ground beef mixture to the slow cooker. Add mushrooms and close the lid. Cook for 7 hours on Low. When the time is done, let the cooked casserole cool slightly.

Nutrition: calories 172, fat 9.5, fiber 0.9, carbs 3.2, protein 18.7

Salmon and Avocado Breakfast Bake
Prep time: 15 minutes | Cooking time: 2 hours | Servings: 4

Ingredients:
- 1 avocado, pitted
- 7 oz salmon fillet
- 2 eggs
- 1 teaspoon ground coriander
- ½ teaspoon salt
- 1 teaspoon butter
- 1 tablespoon almond flour

Directions:
Peel the avocado and chop it. Chop the salmon fillet and sprinkle it with the ground coriander and salt. Beat the eggs in a separate bowl. Add the chopped fish and avocado to the whisked egg and toss together. Then transfer the ingredients to the slow cooker bowl and sprinkle with the almond flour. Stir the ingredients well. Chop the butter and place it in the slow cooker. Close the lid and cook the meal for 2 hours in High. When the salmon avocado bake is cooked, let it cool for 5 minutes and serve!

Nutrition: calories 248, fat 19.5, fiber 4.1, carbs 6, protein 14.9

Broccoli Muffins
Prep time: 15 minutes | Cooking time: 2 hour | Servings: 4

Ingredients:
- 4 eggs, beaten
- ¾ cup almond flour
- 1 teaspoon baking soda
- ¼ teaspoon salt
- 1 teaspoon paprika
- 1 teaspoon turmeric
- 1 tablespoon butter
- 6 oz broccoli, chopped

Directions:
Place the broccoli in the blender and blend it until smooth. Add the beaten eggs, butter, turmeric, paprika, salt, and baking soda to the blender and puree for one minute more. Then transfer the mixture to a big bowl and add almond flour. Stir it well until you get a smooth dough. Pour the dough into muffin molds and place the molds in the slow cooker. Close the lid and cook the muffins for 2 hours on high. Then let the cooked muffins cool slightly.

Nutrition: calories 136, fat 10.1, fiber 2, carbs 5, protein 8

Eggs with Greens

Prep time: 10minutes | Cooking time: 1 hour | Servings: 2

Ingredients:
- 2 eggs, beaten
- 3 oz Italian dark-leaf kale
- ½ teaspoon salt
- 1 teaspoon chili flakes
- 1 tablespoon butter
- 1 tablespoon dried oregano

Directions:
Chop the kale and sprinkle it with the salt, chili flakes, and dried oregano. Chop the butter and place it in the slow cooker. Then make a layer of the chopped kale over the butter. Add the egg and close the lid. Cook the meal for 1 hour on high. When the time is done and the meal is cooked, serve it immediately.

Nutrition: calories 142, fat 10.4, fiber 1.6, carbs 6.3, protein 7.1

Breakfast Bowl

Prep time: 15 minutes | Cooking time: 3 hours | Servings: 4

Ingredients:
- 7 oz chicken fillets, chopped
- 1 tablespoon butter
- 4 eggs, beaten
- 1 teaspoon chili flakes
- 1 teaspoon ground black pepper
- ¾ teaspoon salt
- 1 tablespoon full-fat cream cheese

Directions:
Place the butter and chicken fillets in the slow cooker. Sprinkle the chicken with the chili flakes, ground black pepper, and salt. Whisk the beaten eggs and with the full-fat cream cheese. Stir the mixture and pour it over the chicken. Mix well. Close the lid and cook the breakfast for 3 hours on High. Stir the cooked meal one more time and then transfer to serving bowls.

Nutrition: calories 188, fat 11, fiber 0.2, carbs 0.9, protein 20.5

Keto Egg Muffins

Prep time: 10 minutes | Cooking time: 1 hour | Servings: 4

Ingredients:
- 2 eggs, beaten
- 2 teaspoons butter
- ¼ teaspoon ground black pepper
- 1 teaspoon paprika
- 3 oz bacon, chopped
- 2 oz Parmesan, grated

Directions:
Place the beaten eggs in a blender. Add butter, ground black pepper, and paprika. Blend the mixture for 1 minute on maximum speed. Transfer the egg mixture into the muffin molds. Add chopped bacon. Then sprinkle every muffin with the grated cheese. Transfer the muffin molds into the slow cooker. Cook the muffins for 1 hour on High or until the eggs and bacon in the muffins are cooked (they should be firm to the touch). Serve the breakfast immediately!

Nutrition: calories 211, fat 16.1, fiber 0.2, carbs 1.4, protein 15.3

Brussel Sprouts Eggs

Prep time: 10 minutes | Cooking time: 4 hours | Servings: 2

Ingredients:
- 7 oz Brussel Sprouts
- ½ teaspoon salt
- 1 teaspoon paprika
- 1 tablespoon butter
- 2 eggs

Directions:
Wash Brussel sprouts well then sprinkle them with the salt and paprika. Transfer Brussel sprouts into the slow cooker. Add the butter. Beat the eggs and pour over Brussel sprouts then close the slow cooker. Cook the meal for 4 hours on Low. When the meal is cooked, transfer it to serving plates and

Nutrition: calories 160, fat 10.6, fiber 4.1, carbs 10, protein 9.1

Breakfast Meat Bowl

Prep time: 15 minutes | Cooking time: 3 hours | Servings: 4

Ingredients:
- 4 oz ground chicken
- 4 oz ground beef
- 1 teaspoon tomato puree
- 1 tablespoon butter
- 1 garlic clove, chopped
- 1 teaspoon turmeric
- 1 teaspoon paprika

Directions:
Mix together the ground chicken and ground beef. Sprinkle the meat mixture with the tomato puree and chopped garlic clove. Add turmeric and paprika. Stir the mixture well. Place the butter in the slow cooker and add the ground meat mixture. Close the lid and cook the meal for 3 hours on High. When the meat is cooked, transfer it to serving bowls.

Nutrition: calories 145, fat 6.9, fiber 0.4, carbs 3, protein 17

Egg Bars

Prep time: 15 minutes | Cooking time: 3 hours | Servings: 4

Ingredients:
- 1 green pepper, chopped
- 4 eggs, beaten
- 3 tablespoons almond milk
- 1 tablespoon almond flour
- 1/3 teaspoon cayenne pepper
- 1 teaspoon chili flakes
- 1 tablespoon butter

Directions:
Mix together the whisked eggs and chopped green pepper. Add almond milk and almond flour. Then add cayenne pepper and chili flakes. Stir the mixture well. Then pour the egg mixture into the slow cooker and flatten it with a spatula. Close the lid and cook the meal for 3 hours on High. Let the cooked eggs chill to room temperature. Cut the eggs into bars and serve!

Nutrition: calories 161, fat 13.5, fiber 1.6, carbs 3.9, protein 7.6

Breakfast Turkey Roll

Prep time: 20minutes | Cooking time: 7 hours | Servings: 6

Ingredients:

- 1-pound turkey breast, boneless, skinless
- 1 oz almonds, chopped
- 1 oz celery stalks, chopped
- ½ teaspoon chili flakes
- 2 tablespoons butter
- ¼ teaspoon salt
- 1 tablespoon dill, chopped
- ¾ cup water

Directions:

Beat the turkey breast gently to tenderize. Then sprinkle it with the chili flakes and salt and rub the seasonings into the meat. Mix together the chopped almonds, celery stalk, butter, and chopped dill. Then spread the mixture over the turkey breast. Roll the turkey breast up so that the butter mix in inside. Secure the turkey breast with the toothpicks. Pour water in the slow cooker and place the turkey roll inside with the water, toothpick side down. Close the lid and cook the turkey roll for 7 hours on Low. When the turkey roll is cooked, transfer it to a platter and remove the toothpicks. Slice the turkey roll and

Nutrition: calories 142, fat 7.5, fiber 1.1, carbs 4.6, protein 14.1

Breakfast Bacon and Eggs

Prep time: 10 minutes | Cooking time: 2 hours | Servings: 5

Ingredients:

- 5 eggs, beaten
- 6 oz bacon, chopped
- 1 onion, chopped
- 2 tablespoons butter
- ¼ teaspoon cayenne pepper
- ¾ teaspoon salt

Directions:

Place the chopped bacon in the slow cooker and sprinkle with salt and cayenne pepper. Add butter and cook for 1 hour on High. Then add the chopped onion and stir the mixture. Add the eggs into the slow cooker and close the lid. Cook the meal for 1 hour on High. When the eggs are solid, the meal is cooked.

Nutrition: calories 297, fat 23.2, fiber 0.5, carbs 2.9, protein 18.4

Keto Porridge

Prep time: 8 minutes | Cooking time: 2 hours | Servings: 3

Ingredients:
- 1 tablespoon flaxseed meal
- 3 tablespoons coconut flour
- 1 cup almond milk
- 1 teaspoon stevia
- 1 teaspoon vanilla extract

Directions:
Place the flaxseed meal, coconut flour, vanilla extract, and stevia in the slow cooker. Stir the mixture gently. Then add the almond milk and stir the mixture until homogenous. Close the lid and cook the porridge for 2 hours on Low. Stir the cooked porridge and serve it immediately!

Nutrition: calories 260, fat 21.8, fiber 7.4, carbs 13.3, protein 4.3

Mushroom Omelette

Prep time: 15 minutes | Cooking time: 5 hours | Servings: 3

Ingredients:
- 5 oz mushrooms, chopped
- 1 tablespoon butter
- 1 onion, chopped
- 3 eggs, beaten
- ¼ teaspoon chili flakes

Directions:
Place the chopped mushrooms, butter, and onion in the slow cooker. Add chili flakes and stir the mixture. Close the lid and cook the vegetables for 1 hour on High. Meanwhile, whisk the beaten eggs well. Pour the whisked eggs over the mushroom mixture and close the lid. Cook the omelet for 4 hours on Low. When the omelet is cooked, let it cool slightly. Cut into serving and

Nutrition: calories 122, fat 8.4, fiber 1.3, carbs 5.3, protein 7.5

Western Omelette

Prep time: 15 minutes | Cooking time: 2 hours | Servings: 3

Ingredients:
- 3 eggs, beaten
- 1 tablespoon heavy cream
- ¾ teaspoon salt
- 2 oz Parmesan, shredded
- 1 tablespoon butter
- 3 oz ham, diced
- 1 teaspoon parsley, chopped

Directions:
Mix together the beaten eggs and heavy cream. Add salt and butter. Whisk the mixture until smooth. Add diced ham and chopped parsley. Pour the whisked egg mixture in the slow cooker and sprinkle it with the shredded cheese. Close the lid and cook the omelet for 2 hours on High. When the time is done, let the cooked meal chill until room temperature.

Nutrition: calories 221, fat 16.6, fiber 0.4, carbs 2.3, protein 16.5

Slow Cooker Sausages

Prep time: 25 minutes | Cooking time: 3 hours | Servings: 4

Ingredients:
- 10 oz ground chicken
- 1 teaspoon minced garlic
- ¾ teaspoon chili flakes
- 1 teaspoon ground black pepper
- 1 tablespoon almond flour
- 1 egg yolk
- 1 tablespoon butter

Directions:
Mix together the ground chicken and minced garlic. Add chili flakes and ground black pepper. Add almond flour and egg yolk. Stir the ground chicken mixture well. Then chop the butter and place it in the slow cooker. Make medium sausages by forming them with your hands then freeze them for 15 minutes. After this, place the sausages in the slow cooker and cook for 3 hours on High. When the sausages are cooked, transfer them onto the serving platter.

Nutrition: calories 266, fat 12.8, fiber 0.9, carbs 2.2, 22.8

Coconut Porridge

Prep time: 10 minutes | Cooking time: 4 hours | Servings: 4

Ingredients:
- 2 eggs
- 4 tablespoons butter
- 2 tablespoons coconut flour
- 1 teaspoon stevia extract
- 7 tablespoons coconut cream
- 1 teaspoon vanilla extract

Directions:
Mix up together the coconut flour, stevia extract, coconut cream, and vanilla extract. Add butter and beat the eggs into the mixture. Stir everything with a hand mixer until smooth. Then transfer the mixture to the slow cooker. Cook the meal for 4 hours on Low. When the time is done, stir the cooked porridge gently with a spoon

Nutrition: calories 227, fat 21, fiber 3.1, carbs 5.8, protein 4.5

Salmon Cutlets

Prep time: 15 minutes | Cooking time: 2 hours | Servings: 2

Ingredients:
- 8 oz salmon fillet, chopped
- 1 garlic clove, chopped
- 1 oz onion, chopped
- 1 tablespoon almond flour
- 1 tablespoon coconut flour
- 1/3 teaspoon ground black pepper
- ¾ teaspoon salt
- 1 tablespoon butter

Directions:
Mix up together the chopped salmon fillet, garlic, and onion. Add ground black pepper and salt then stir the mixture well. Add the almond flour and coconut flour. Stir the mixture well. Form medium cutlets from the fish mixture. Put the butter in the slow cooker then place the fish cutlets in the slow cooker as well. Close the lid and cook the cutlets for 2 hours on High. Then transfer the cooked salmon cutlets to a serving plate and

Nutrition: calories 305, fat 20.2, fiber 3.4, carbs 7.6, protein 25.9

Bacon Beef Casserole

Prep time: 25 minutes | Cooking time: 8 hours | Servings: 5

Ingredients:
- 1 teaspoon ghee
- 1 garlic clove, chopped
- 1 onion, chopped
- 7 oz ground beef
- 6 oz bacon, sliced
- 1 tablespoon tomato puree
- 1 teaspoon salt
- 1 tablespoon butter
- 1 teaspoon cayenne pepper
- ½ teaspoon ground black pepper

Directions:
Mix together the chopped garlic and onion. Add ground beef and tomato puree. Add salt, cayenne pepper, and ground black pepper and stir the mixture well. Put the ghee in the slow cooker. Place the meat mixture in the slow cooker and press the butter into the meat. Cover the ground meat mixture with the sliced bacon and close the lid. Cook the casserole for 8 hours on Low. Let the dish cool for 15 minutes. Serve it!

Nutrition: calories 315, fat19.9, fiber0.6, carbs 3.1, protein 25

Breakfast Tender Chicken Strips

Prep time: 15 minutes | Cooking time: 5 hours | Servings: 5

Ingredients:
- 1-pound chicken fillets
- 2 tablespoons butter
- 1 teaspoon dried dill
- 1 teaspoon dried oregano
- 1 teaspoon dried parsley
- 2 tablespoons full-fat cream

Directions:
Cut the chicken fillets into the strips. Then sprinkle the chicken strips with the dried dill, oregano, and parsley. Toss the poultry with the full-fat cream. Place the butter in the slow cooker and add the chicken strips. Then close the lid and cook the chicken strips for 5 hours on Low. Stir the cooked chicken strips and transfer onto a serving platter.

Nutrition: calories 222, fat 12.1, fiber 0.2, carbs 0.6, protein 26.6

Chicken Muffins

Prep time: 20 minutes | Cooking time: 5 hours | Servings: 2

Ingredients:
- 5 oz ground chicken
- 1 tablespoon coconut flour
- 1 teaspoon minced garlic
- ½ teaspoon chili flakes
- 1 tablespoon butter
- 1 egg, beaten

Directions:
Mix the ground chicken and coconut flour. Add minced garlic and chili flakes. Stir the mixture gently and add the egg. Mix until homogenous. Then transfer the mixture into individual muffin molds and put a small amount of the butter in every muffin. Put the muffins in the slow cooker and cook for 5 hours on Low. Cool the cooked muffins.

Nutrition: calories 234, fat 13.6, fiber 1.5, carbs 3.2, protein 23.9

Vanilla Pancakes

Prep time: 15 minutes | Cooking time: 2 hours | Servings: 6

Ingredients:
- 1 cup coconut flour
- 2 eggs, beaten
- 1 teaspoon baking powder
- 1 tablespoon vanilla extract
- 1 tablespoon ghee
- ½ cup almond milk
- ¾ teaspoon salt
- ¼ teaspoon nutmeg

Directions:
Whisk the eggs with the coconut flour and baking powder in the mixing bowl. Add vanilla extract and ghee. Then add milk, salt, and nutmeg. Stir the pancake mixture carefully until smooth. Pour the pancake batter into the slow cooker and close the lid. Cook the pancake for 2 hours on High. When the pancake is cooked, cut it into servings and serve.

Nutrition: calories 173, fat 10.4, fiber 8.5, carbs 15.3, protein 5

Veggie Turkey Smash

Prep time: 15 minutes | Cooking time: 7 hours | Servings: 4

Ingredients:
- 1 eggplant
- 1 onion
- 9 oz ground turkey
- 1 green pepper, chopped
- 1 tablespoon butter
- 1 teaspoon chili flakes

Directions:
Peel the eggplant and onion and chop both into small pieces. Then combine the chopped vegetables with the green pepper. Add butter, chili flakes, and ground turkey. Mix and transfer to the slow cooker. Cook the turkey smash for 7 hours on Low. When the time is done, stir the cooked meal carefully and transfer to serving bowls.

Nutrition: calories 196, fat 10.2, fiber 5.2, carbs 10.7, protein 19.2

Paprika Shrimp

Prep time: 10 minutes | Cooking time: 1 hour | Servings: 6

Ingredients:
- 1-pound shrimp, peeled
- ¼ teaspoon ground black pepper
- 1 teaspoon paprika
- ¼ teaspoon minced garlic
- ¾ cup chicken stock

Directions:
Sprinkle the peeled shrimp with the ground black pepper and paprika. Then sprinkle the shrimp with the mincedgarlic and stir well. Place the chicken stock in the slow cooker. Add the seasoned shrimp and close the lid. Cook the shrimp for 1 hour on High. Then transfer the shrimps to the serving plate and serve!

Nutrition: calories 92, fat 1.4, fiber 0.2, carbs 1.5, protein 17.4

Breakfast Pizza

Prep time: 15 minutes | Cooking time: 3 hours | Servings: 4

Ingredients:
- 4 tablespoons almond flour
- ½ teaspoon baking powder
- ¾ teaspoon salt
- 2 eggs, beaten
- 4 oz ham, chopped
- 1 teaspoon Italian seasoning
- 1 teaspoon olive oil
- 3 oz Parmesan, grated

Directions:
Mix the almond flour and baking powder. Add salt and beaten eggs and knead the dough. Roll out the dough with a rolling pin. Spray the slow cooker bowl with the olive oil. Place the rolled out dough in the slow cooker. Sprinkle the dough with the chopped ham and grated Parmesan. Then sprinkle the pizza with the Italian seasoning. Close the lid and cook the pizza for 3 hours on High. Then let the cooked pizza cool slightly and serve it!

Nutrition: calories 320, fat 24.7, fiber 3.4, carbs 8.5, protein 20.3

Breakfast Sweet Pepper Hash

Prep time: 15 minutes | Cooking time: 4 hours | Servings: 4

Ingredients:
- 8 oz ground pork
- 1 onion, chopped
- 2 sweet peppers, chopped
- 1 teaspoon ghee
- ¼ cup chicken stock
- ½ teaspoon chili flakes
- 4 oz Cheddar cheese

Directions:
Mix the chopped onion and sweet pepper. Add chickens stock and ghee. Add the chili flakes and transfer the mix to the slow cooker. Shred the cheddar cheese and add it to the slow cooker as well. Add ground pork and stir the ingredients carefully with a spatula. Close the lid and cook the hash for 4 hours on High. Stir the meal and serve!

Nutrition: calories 235, fat 12.7, fiber 1.4, carbs 7.5, protein 22.8

Pork Breakfast Sausages

Prep time: 15 minutes | Cooking time: 7 hours | Servings: 3

Ingredients:
- 9 oz ground pork
- 1 oz onion, grated
- 1 tablespoon almond flour
- 1 teaspoon coconut flour
- ¼ teaspoon ground black pepper
- ¾ teaspoon chili flakes
- 1 teaspoon ghee

Directions:
Mix up together the ground pork and grated onion. Add almond flour and coconut flour. Then add ground black pepper and chili flakes. Stir the mixture well and form small sausages. Place the sausages in the slow cooker and add the ghee. Cook the sausages for 7 hours on Low. When the sausages are cooked, let them cool slightly.

Nutrition: calories 188, fat 9.8, fiber 2.9, carbs 5.7, protein 25.1

Chicken Bites

Prep time: 15 minutes | Cooking time: 2 hours | Servings: 2

Ingredients:
- 10 oz chicken fillet
- 1 egg
- 1 teaspoon olive oil
- 3 tablespoons almond flour
- ½ teaspoon ground paprika
- ½ teaspoon salt

Directions:
Cut the chicken fillet into medium pieces and beat gently to tenderize. Beat the egg in a separate bowl. Mix up together the whisked egg, salt and ground paprika. Toss the chicken in the whisked egg mixture. After this, coat the chicken bites in the almond flour. Pour the olive oil in the slow cooker and add the chicken bites. Close the lid and cook the chicken bites for 2 hours on High. Serve the meal immediately!

Nutrition: calories 281, fat 18, fiber 2.4, carbs 4.7, protein 26.4

Avocado Boats

Prep time: 15 minutes | Cooking time: 2 hours | Servings: 2

Ingredients:
- 2 eggs, whisked
- 1 avocado, pitted, halved
- ¾ teaspoon ground black pepper
- ¾ teaspoon salt
- 2 teaspoons butter

Directions:
Place the avocado halves in the slow cooker. Put the butter in both holes of the avocado halves. Then pour the eggs into the avocado holes. Sprinkle the eggs with the ground black pepper and salt. Close the lid and cook the boats for 2 hours on High. When the eggs are cooked, serve the avocado boats hot.

Nutrition: calories 304, fat 27.8, fiber 6.9, carbs 9.5, protein 7.6

Cabbage Rolls

Prep time: 20 minutes | Cooking time: 7 hours | Servings: 4

Ingredients:
- 4 oz white cabbage, leaves
- 5 oz ground chicken
- ¼ teaspoon salt
- 1 teaspoon ground black pepper
- ½ teaspoon butter
- ¾ cup chicken stock
- 4 oz mushrooms, chopped

Directions:
Roll out the cabbage leaves gently with the help of the rolling pin to flatten them. Then place the ground chicken and salt in a mixing bowl. Add the ground black pepper and chopped mushrooms and stir. Place a little of the ground chicken mixture on each cabbage leaf and roll them up to enclose the chicken in the cabbage. Put the cabbage rolls in the slow cooker. Add chicken stock and close the lid. Cook the cabbage rolls for 7 hours on Low. When the cabbage rolls are cooked, let them chill for 15 minutes and serve!

Nutrition: calories 88, fat 3.4, fiber 1.1, carbs 3.1, protein 11.7

Collard Greens

Prep time: 10 minutes | Cooking time: 4 hours | Servings: 3

Ingredients:
- 8 oz collard greens, chopped
- 1 green pepper, chopped
- 1 onion, diced
- ¼ cup chicken stock
- 1 tablespoon butter
- 1 teaspoon turmeric
- ¼ teaspoon thyme

Directions:
Place the collard greens, chopped green pepper, and diced onion in the slow cooker. Add chicken stock and butter. Add turmeric and thyme. Stir the ingredients and close the id. Cook the mealfor 4 hours on Low. When the time is done, all the ingredients should be soft and tender. Serve the breakfast immediately!

Nutrition: calories 81, fat 4.6, fiber 4.1, carbs 10, protein 2.6

Breakfast Pie

Prep time: 25 minutes | Cooking time: 7 hours | Servings: 6

Ingredients:
- 1 eggs
- 4 tablespoons almond milk
- ½ cup coconut flour
- ¾ teaspoon salt
- 5 oz cauliflower, chopped
- ½ onion, chopped
- 1 teaspoon butter
- 1 tablespoon full-fat cream
- 1 teaspoon turmeric
- 4 oz Parmesan, grated
- 5 oz ground chicken

Directions:
Beat the egg in the bowl and whisk well. Add almond milk and coconut flour. Then add salt and butter. Stir the mixture and knead into a smooth dough. Add more flour if needed. Then place the dough in the slow cooker and push the dough along the bottom and halfway up the sides of the slow cooker bowl to make the pie crust. Place the chopped cauliflower, onion, and grated parmesan on top of the pie crust. Add full-fat cream and turmeric. Then add ground chicken and close the lid. Cook the pie for 7 hours on Low. Chill the cooked pie little and then cut into slices. Serve!

Nutrition: calories 199, fat 10.9, fiber 5.1, carbs 10.4, protein 16.1

Cod Bites

Prep time: 15 minutes | Cooking time: 4 hours | Servings: 3

Ingredients:
- 10 oz cod fillet
- 2 tablespoons almond flour
- 1 teaspoon garlic powder
- 2 eggs, beaten
- 1 teaspoon ghee

Directions:
Cut the cod fillet into the medium squares. Sprinkle the cod fillets with the garlic powder. Then dip them in the beaten eggs. Transfer the cod fillets onto a plate and coat the fillets on all sides with the almond flour. Put the ghee in the slow cooker and add the cod fillets. Cook the cod bites for 4 hours on Low. When the cod bites are cooked, chill them a little and serve!

Nutrition: calories 240, fat 14.5, fiber 2.1, carbs 4.9, protein 24.7

Moroccan Meatballs

Prep time: 15 minutes | Cooking time: 6 hours | Servings: 4

Ingredients:
- 1 teaspoon paprika
- 1 teaspoon turmeric
- ¾ teaspoon ground black pepper
- ½ teaspoon salt
- 1 egg
- 1 tablespoon butter
- 4 tablespoons chicken stock
- 10 oz ground beef
- 1 teaspoon garlic powder

Directions:
Mix the paprika, turmeric, ground black pepper, and salt. Beat the egg into the spice mixture and stir well. Add butter and ground beef. Then add the garlic powder and stir until you get a well blended meatball mixture. Form medium meatballs with your hands and place them in the slow cooker. Add the chicken stock and close the lid. Cook the meatballs for 6 hours on Low. When the meatballs are cooked, serve them immediately!

Nutrition: calories 180, fat 8.6, fiber 0.5, carbs 1.6, protein 23.2

Breakfast Shredded Pork

Prep time: 15 minutes | Cooking time: 10 hours | Servings: 5

Ingredients:
- 1-pound pork chops
- 1 cup chicken stock
- 1 teaspoon thyme
- 1 garlic clove
- 1 teaspoon salt
- 1 teaspoon full-fat cream

Directions:
Sprinkle the pork chops with the thyme and salt. Chop the garlic clove and place it in the slow cooker. Add full-fat cream and pork chops. Then add the chicken stock and closethe lid. Cook the pork chops for 10 hours on low. When the time is done, transfer all the content of the slow cooker to a big bowl. Shred the pork with forks and serve it!

Nutrition: calories 295, fat 22.8, fiber 0.1, carbs 0.5, protein 20.6

Bacon Pecan Bok Choy

Prep time: 15 minutes | Cooking time: 4 hours | Servings: 4

Ingredients:
- 12 oz bok choy, chopped
- 1 tablespoon olive oil
- 6 oz bacon, chopped
- 1 oz pecans, chopped
- 4 tablespoons beef broth
- ¼ teaspoon salt

Directions:
Put the chopped bacon in slow cooker. Add salt and olive oil. Stir it gently and cook for 1 hour on High. Add the chopped bok choy and pecans. Close the lid and cook the meal for another 3 hours on Low. Stir and serve it!

Nutrition: calories 323, fat 26.6, fiber 1.6, carbs 3.5, protein 18.1

Chia Seeds Pudding

Prep time: 8 minutes | Cooking time: 1 hour | Servings: 4

Ingredients:
- ½ cup chia seeds
- 1 cup almond milk
- 1 teaspoon stevia extract
- 1 teaspoon vanilla extract
- 1 teaspoon butter

Directions:
Place the chia seeds, almond milk, stevia extract, and vanilla extract in the slow cooker. Add butter and stir gently. Close the lid and cook the meal for 1 hour on Low. Stir the pudding and serve immediately.

Nutrition: calories 253, fat 21.8, fiber 8.6, carbs 12.4, protein 4.9

Prosciutto Chicken Nuggets

Prep time: 15 minutes | Cooking time: 3 hours | Servings: 3

Ingredients:
- 6 oz Prosciutto, sliced
- 8 oz chicken fillet
- 1 teaspoon paprika
- 1 teaspoon chili flakes
- 1 tablespoon ghee
- 2 tablespoons chicken stock

Directions:
Sprinkle the chicken fillet with the paprika and chili flakes. Then cut the chicken fillet into the small pieces. Wrap the chicken pieces with Prosciutto and place in the slow cooker. Add ghee and chicken stock and close the lid. Cook the chicken nuggets for 3 hours on High.

Nutrition: calories 266, fat 13.1, fiber 0.3, carbs 1.3, protein 33.9

Avocado Tuna Balls

Prep time: 15 minutes | Cooking time: 2 hours | Servings: 4

Ingredients:
- 1 avocado, pitted, peeled
- 2 tablespoons coconut flour
- 1 teaspoon salt
- 6 oz tuna
- 1 egg
- 1 teaspoon olive oil
- 1 tablespoon coconut flakes, unsweetened

Directions:
Chop tuna into tiny pieces. Mash the avocado and combine it with the chopped tuna. Beat the egg into the mixture and add the salt. Stir well. Make small balls and sprinkle them with the coconut flakes and coconut flour. Pour the olive oil in the slow cooker. Add the tuna balls and close the lid. Cook the meal for 2 hours on High. Serve the cooked meal hot!

Nutrition: calories 242, fat 16.9, fiber 6, carbs 8.6, protein 14.7

Basil Meatballs

Prep time: 15 minutes | Cooking time: 5 hours | Servings: 4

Ingredients:
- 1 oz basil, chopped
- 7 oz ground beef
- 1 tablespoons coconut flakes, unsweetened
- 1 teaspoon paprika
- 1 egg yolk
- 1 tablespoon butter
- 1 teaspoon curry seasoning

Directions:
Mix the choppedbasil and ground beef. Add paprika and coconut flakes. Add the egg yolk and curry. Stir the meat mixture until well blended. Form small meatballs and place them in the slow cooker. Add butter and close the lid. Cook the meat basil balls for 5 hours on Low. Then transfer the mealto plates and

Nutrition: calories 140, fat 7.7, fiber 0.6, carbs 1.1, protein 16.2

Kale Frittata

Prep time: 15 minutes | Cooking time: 2 hours | Servings: 3

Ingredients:
- 3 oz Italian dark leaf kale, chopped
- 2 eggs
- ¾ cup almond milk
- 1 tablespoon butter
- 1 teaspoon paprika

Directions:

Beat the eggs in a mixing bowl. Add paprika and almond milk. Stir well then add the chopped kale. Place the butter in the slow cooker and add the egg mixture. Close the lid and cook frittata for 2 hours on High. Chill the cooked frittata slightly and serve!

Nutrition: calories 230, fat 21.2., fiber 2, carbs 6.9, protein 6.1

Main Dishes

Keto Lasagna

Prep time: 20 minutes | Cooking time: 7 hours | Servings: 6

Ingredients:
- 10 oz ground beef
- 1 tablespoons tomato puree
- 1 zucchini
- 5 oz Parmesan, grated
- 1 tablespoon butter
- ½ teaspoon salt
- 1 teaspoon paprika
- 1 teaspoon chili flakes
- 1 tablespoon full-fat heavy cream

Directions:
Slice the zucchini lengthwise. Mix the ground beef, salt, paprika, and chili flakes. Then mix the full-fat cream and tomato puree. Chop the butter and put it in the slow cooker. Make a layer of the zucchini in the bottom of the slow cooker bowl. Put a layer of the ground beef mixture on top of the zucchini layer. After this repeat, the same layers until you use all the ingredients. Sprinkle the lasagna with the grated Parmesan and close the lid. Cook the lasagna for 7 hours on Low. Chill the cooked meal little and serve!

Nutrition: calories 197, fat 11, fiber 0.5, carbs 2.5, protein 22.5

Butter Chicken

Prep time: 15minutes | Cooking time: 3 hours | Servings: 4

Ingredients:
- 4 tablespoons butter
- 3 oz spinach, chopped
- 1 teaspoon onion powder
- 1 teaspoon paprika
- 12 oz chicken breast, skinless, boneless
- ½ teaspoon salt
- ¼ cup chicken stock

Directions:
Beat the chicken breasts gently to tenderize and sprinkle it with the salt and paprika. Then place the butter and spinach in a blender. Add onion powder and blend the mixture for 1 minute at high speed. Spread the chicken breast with the butter mixture on each side. Place the buttered chicken in the slow cooker and the chicken stock. Close the lid and cook the chicken for 3 hours on Low. Serve the chicken immediately!

Nutrition: calories 208, fat 13.9, fiber 0.7, carbs 1.6, protein 18.9

Tuscan Chicken

Prep time: 15 minutes | Cooking time: 7 hours | Servings: 8

Ingredients:
- 1-pound chicken breast, skinless, boneless
- 1 tablespoon olive oil
- ½ cup full-fat cream
- 1 oz spinach, chopped
- 3 oz Parmesan, grated
- 1 teaspoon chili flakes
- ½ teaspoon paprika
- 1 teaspoon minced garlic
- ½ teaspoon ground black pepper

Directions:

Chop the chicken breast roughly and sprinkle it with the chili flakes, paprika, minced garlic, and ground black pepper. Stir the chicken and transfer to the slow cooker. Add the full-fat cream and olive oil. Add spinach and grated cheese. Stir the chicken gently and close the lid. Cook the chicken for 7 hours on Low. Transfer cooked Tuscan chicken on the serving plates and serve!

Nutrition: calories 136, fat 7.2, fiber 0.2, carbs 1.4, protein 16

Corned Beef

Prep time: 10 minutes | Cooking time: 8 hours | Servings: 6

Ingredients:
- 1-pound corned beef
- 1 teaspoon peppercorns
- 1 teaspoon chili flakes
- 1 teaspoon mustard seeds
- 1 bay leaf
- 1 teaspoon salt
- 1 oz bacon fat
- 4 garlic cloves
- 1 cup water
- 1 tablespoon butter

Directions:

Mix the peppercorns, chili flakes, mustard seeds, and salt in the bowl. Then rub the corned beef with the spice mixture well. Peel the garlic and place it in the slow cooker. Add the corned beef. Add water, butter, and bay leaf. Add the bacon fat and close the lid. Cook the corned beef for 8 hours on Low. When the corned beef is cooked, discard the bay leaf then transfer the beef to a plate and cut into servings.

Nutrition: calories 178, fat 13.5, fiber 0.3, carbs 1.3, protein 12.2

Sardine Pate

Prep time: 15 minutes | Cooking time: 3 hours | Servings: 6

Ingredients:
- ½ cup water
- 3 tablespoons butter
- 1 teaspoon onion powder
- 1 teaspoon dried parsley
- 12 oz sardine fillets, chopped

Directions:
Put the chopped sardine fillets, dried parsley, onion powder, and water in the slow cooker. Close the lid and cook the fish for 3 hours on Low. Strain the sardine fillet and put it in a blender. Add butter and blend the mixture for 3 minutes on high speed. Transfer the cooked pate into serving bowls and serve!

Nutrition: calories 170, fat 12.3, fiber 0, carbs 0.3, protein 14.1

Spare Ribs

Prep time: 10 minutes | Cooking time: 8 hours | Servings: 6

Ingredients:
- 1-pound pork loin ribs
- 1 teaspoon olive oil
- 1 teaspoon minced garlic
- ¼ teaspoon cumin
- ¼ teaspoon chili powder
- 1 tablespoon butter
- 5 tablespoons water

Directions:
Mix the olive oil, minced garlic, cumin, and chili flakes in a bowl. Melt the butter and add tothe spice mixture. Stir it well and add water. Stir again. Then rub the pork ribs with the spice mixture generously and place the ribs in the slow cooker. Close the lid and cook the ribs for 8 hours on Low. When the ribs are cooked, serve them immediately!

Nutrition: calories 203, fat 14.1, fiber 0.6, carbs 10, protein 9.8

Pork Shoulder

Prep time: 25 minutes | Cooking time: 7 hours | Servings: 6

Ingredients:
- 1-pound pork shoulder
- 2 cups water
- 1 onion, peeled
- 2 garlic cloves, peeled
- 1 teaspoon peppercorns
- 1 teaspoon chili flakes
- ½ teaspoon paprika
- 1 teaspoon turmeric
- 1 teaspoon cumin

Directions:
Sprinkle the pork shoulder with the peppercorns, chili flakes, paprika, turmeric, and cumin. Stir it well and let it sit for 15 minutes to marinate. Transfer the pork shoulder to the slow cooker. Add water and peeled the onion. Add garlic cloves and close the lid. Cook the pork shoulder for 7 hours on Low. Remove the pork shoulder from the slow cooker and serve!

Nutrition: calories 234, fat 16.4, fiber 0.7, carbs 2.8, protein 18

Lamb Chops

Prep time: 15 minutes | Cooking time: 3 hours | Servings: 2

Ingredients:
- 10 oz lamb chops
- 1 tablespoon tomato puree
- ½ teaspoon cumin
- ½ teaspoon ground coriander
- 1 teaspoon garlic powder
- 1 teaspoon butter
- 5 tablespoons water

Directions:

Mix the tomato puree, cumin, ground coriander, garlic powder, and water in the bowl. Brush the lamb chops with the tomato puree mixture on each side and let marinate for 20 minutes. Toss the butter in the slow cooker. Add the lamb chops and close the lid. Cook the lamb chops for 3 hours on High. Transfer the cooked lamb onto serving plates and

Nutrition: calories 290, fat 12.5, fiber 0.4, carbs 2, protein 40.3

Rosemary Leg of Lamb

Prep time: 15 minutes | Cooking time: 7 hours | Servings: 8

Ingredients:
- 2-pound leg of lamb
- 1 onion
- 3 cups water
- 1 garlic clove, peeled
- 1 tablespoon mustard seeds
- 1 teaspoon salt
- ½ teaspoon turmeric
- 1 teaspoon ground black pepper

Directions:

Chop the garlic clove and combine it with the mustard seeds, turmeric, black pepper and salt. Peel the onion and grate it. Mix the grated onion and spice mixture. Rub the leg of lamb with the grated onion mixture. Put the leg of lamb in the slow cooker and cook it for 7 hours on Low. Serve the cooked meal!

Nutrition: calories 225, fat 8.7, fiber 0.6, carbs 2.2, protein 32.4

Creamy Chicken Thighs

Prep time: 15 minutes | Cooking time: 6 hours | Servings: 4

Ingredients:
- 1-pound chicken thighs, skinless
- ¼ cup almond milk, unsweetened
- 1 tablespoon full-fat cream cheese
- 1 teaspoon salt
- 1 onion, diced
- 1 teaspoon paprika

Directions:
Mix the almond milk and full-fat cream. Add salt, diced onion, and paprika. Stir the mixture well. Place the chicken thighs in the slow cooker. Add the almond milk mixture and stir it gently. Close the slow cooker lid and cook the chicken thighs for 6 hours on High. Transfer the cooked chicken heart in the serving bowls and serve immediately!

Nutrition: calories 224, fat 14.3, fiber 1.1, carbs 4.7, protein 18.9

Peppered Steak

Prep time: 15 minutes | Cooking time: 4 hours | Servings: 4

Ingredients:
- 10 oz Sirloin Steak
- 3 cups water
- 1 tablespoon peppercorns
- 1 teaspoon salt
- ½ teaspoon ground nutmeg
- 2 garlic cloves, peeled
- 1 teaspoon olive oil

Directions:
Make the small cuts in the sirlion and chop the garlic cloves roughly. Place the garlic cloves in the sirloin cuts. Sprinkle the steak with the salt, ground nutmeg, and peppercorns. Transfer the steak in the slow cooker and add water. Close the lid and cook the steak for 4 hours on Low. Then remove the steak from the slow cooker and slice it.

Nutrition: calories 192, fat 12, fiber 4, carbs 1, protein 12

Rabbit Stew

Prep time: 15 minutes | Cooking time: 5 hours | Servings: 6

Ingredients:
- 2 eggplants, chopped
- 1 zucchini, chopped
- 1 onion, chopped
- 10 oz rabbit, chopped
- 2 cups water
- 1 tablespoon butter
- 1 teaspoon salt
- 1 teaspoon chili flakes

Directions:
Place the chopped eggplants, zucchini, onion, and rabbit in the slow cooker. Add water, butter, salt, and chili flakes. Stir the stew gently and close the lid. Cook the stew for 5 hours on Low. Then let the cooked rabbit stew cool slightly then serve it!

Nutrition: calories 168, fat 6.1, fiber 7.2, carbs 13.6, protein 16.1

Duck Breast

Prep time: 10 minutes | Cooking time: 5 hours | Servings: 4

Ingredients:
- 1 teaspoon liquid stevia
- 1-pound duck breast, boneless, skinless
- 1 teaspoon chili pepper
- 2 tablespoons butter
- ½ cup water
- 1 bay leaf

Directions:
Rub the duck breast with the chili pepper and liquid stevia then transfer it to the slow cooker. Add the bay leaf and water. Add butter and close the lid. Cook the duck breast for 5 hours on Low. Let the cooked duck breast rest for 10 minutes then remove it from the slow cooker. Slice it into the servings.

Nutrition: calories 199 fat 10.3, fiber 0.1, carbs 0.3, protein 25.1

Jerk Chicken

Prep time: 25 minutes | Cooking time: 5 hours | Servings: 4

Ingredients:
- 1 teaspoon nutmeg
- 1 teaspoon cinnamon
- 1 teaspoon minced garlic
- ½ teaspoon cloves
- 1 teaspoon ground coriander
- 1 tablespoon Erythritol
- 1-pound chicken thighs
- ½ cup water
- 1 tablespoon butter

Directions:
Mix the nutmeg, cinnamon, minced garlic, cloves, and ground coriander. Add Erythritol and stir the ingredients until well blended. Sprinkle the chicken thighs with the spice mixture. Let the chicken thighs sit for 10 minutes to marinate then put thechicken thighs in the slow cooker. Add the butter and water. Close the lid and cook Jerk chicken for 5 hours on Low. Serve Jerk chicken immediately!

Nutrition: calories 247, fat 11.5, fiber 0.5, carbs 4.9, protein 33

Balsamic Beef

Prep time: 20 minutes | Cooking time: 7 hours | Servings: 4

Ingredients:
- 2 tablespoons balsamic vinegar
- 1 tablespoon olive oil
- 1-pound beef loin
- 1 teaspoon minced garlic
- ½ teaspoon ground coriander
- 1 teaspoon cumin
- ½ teaspoon dried dill
- 2 tablespoons water

Directions:
Chop the beef loin roughly and place it in a large bowl then sprinkle it with the balsamic vinegar. Add olive oil, minced garlic, ground coriander, cumin, and dried dill. Stir the meat well and let sit for 10 minutes. Place the meat in the slow cooker and add water. Close the lid and cook the beef for 7 hours on Low. When the beef is tender, it is cooked!

Nutrition: calories 241, fat 13.1, fiber 0.1, carbs 0.6, protein 30.5

Beef Curry

Prep time: 15 minutes | Cooking time: 8 hours | Servings: 4

Ingredients:
- 11 oz beefsteak
- 1 tablespoon curry paste
- 1 teaspoon salt
- ½ teaspoon chili pepper
- 1 teaspoon paprika
- ½ cup water
- 1 teaspoon dried mint
- 1 onion, diced
- 1 teaspoon butter
- ¼ teaspoon peppercorns

Directions:
Mix the curry paste and salt. Add chili pepper and paprika. Add the dried mint and butter. Add peppercorns and mix until homogenous. Mix the curry and water. Pour the curry mixture into the slow cooker. Add dicedonion and beefsteak. Close the lid and cook the beef curry for 8 hours on Low. Cut the cooked beefsteak on the servings and serve it!

Nutrition: calories 192, fat 8.1, fiber 0.9, carbs 4.1, protein 24.3

Keto Chili

Prep time: 10 minutes | Cooking time: 3 hours | Servings: 6

Ingredients:
- 8 oz ground beef
- 2 cups spinach, chopped
- 1 tablespoon tomato puree
- 1 bell pepper, chopped
- 1 onion, diced
- ½ teaspoon ground coriander
- 1 teaspoon ground black pepper
- 1 teaspoon chili pepper
- ½ garlic clove, diced
- 1 cup water
- 1 teaspoon butter

Directions:
Mix the ground beef, chopped spinach, tomato puree, diced onion, ground coriander, ground black pepper, chili pepper and diced onion. Stir the mixture until well blended and transfer it to a slow cooker. Add water and butter. Close the lid and cook the chili for 3 hours on High. Cool the cooked chili slightly and serve!

Nutrition: calories 94, fat 3.1, fiber 1.1, carbs 4.2, protein 12.3

Ground Pork Bowl

Prep time: 10 minutes | Cooking time: 2 hours | Servings: 4

Ingredients:
- 9 oz ground pork
- 2 bell peppers, chopped
- 1 onion, diced
- 1 tablespoon butter
- 1 teaspoon chili pepper
- ½ teaspoon cayenne pepper
- 1 teaspoon salt
- ¼ cup water

Directions:
Place the ground pork, chopped bell peppers, and diced onion in the slow cooker. Add butter, chili pepper, cayenne pepper, and salt. Stir the meat mixture with a spatula. Add water and close the slow cooker lid. Cook the ground pork for 2 hours on High. Transfer the cooked ground pork in the serving bowls and serve!

Nutrition: calories 148, fat 5.4, fiber 1.5, carbs 7.3, protein 17.7

Chili Verde

Prep time: 15 minutes | Cooking time: 4 hours | Servings: 4

Ingredients:
- 1-pound pork loin
- ½ teaspoon cumin
- ½ teaspoon ground coriander
- ½ teaspoon chili flakes
- 1 garlic clove, peeled
- 1 cup water
- ½ cup Keto green chili (no sugar added)

Directions:
Chop the pork loin roughly and place it in the slow cooker. Add cumin, ground coriander, and chili flakes. Add the garlic clove and Keto green chili. Stir the ingredients and add water. Close the lid and cook chili Verde for 4 hours on Low. Serve the cooked meal immediately!

Nutrition: calories 287, fat 15.9, fiber 0.1, carbs 2.4, protein 31.1

Marinated Greek Style Pork

Prep time: 30 minutes | Cooking time: 2 hours | Servings: 4

Ingredients:
- 12 oz pork chops
- 4 teaspoons full-fat cream
- 1 teaspoon ground black pepper
- 1 tablespoon olive oil
- 1 teaspoon dried oregano
- 1 teaspoon dried mint
- ½ teaspoon thyme
- 1 tablespoon butter
- 1 cup water

Directions:
Rub the pork chops with the full-fat cream, ground black pepper, olive oil, dried oregano, dried mint, and thyme. Let it sit for 20 minutes to marinate. Transfer the pork chops in the slow cooker and add butter and water. Close the lid and cook the pork chops for 2 hours on High. Serve the cooked meat immediately!

Nutrition: calories 333, fat 27.8, fiber 0.4, carbs 0.8, protein 19.3

Shredded Chicken

Prep time: 15 minutes | Cooking time: 4 hours | Servings: 4

Ingredients:
- 1-pound chicken breast, boneless, skinless
- 1 teaspoon turmeric
- 1 tablespoon butter
- 2 cups water
- 1 teaspoon salt
- ½ teaspoon ground nutmeg

Directions:
Chop the chicken roughly and sprinkle it with the turmeric, salt, and ground nutmeg. Place the chicken in the slow cooker and toss together with the spices. Add water and butter. Close the lid and cook the poultry for 4hourson Low. Transfer the cooked chicken to a bowl and shred with 2 forks. Serve the cooked shredded chicken immediately!

Nutrition: calories 158, fat 5.9, fiber 0.2, carbs 0.5, protein 24.1

Keto Beef Ribs

Prep time: 15 minutes | Cooking time: 5 hours | Servings: 4

Ingredients:
- 10 oz beef ribs
- 1 onion, grated
- ½ cup water
- 1 teaspoon ground nutmeg
- ½ teaspoon chili pepper
- 1 teaspoon turmeric
- 1 tablespoon olive oil
- 1 garlic clove, peeled
- 1 tomato, chopped

Directions:
Mix the grated onion, ground nutmeg, chili pepper, turmeric, and olive oil in a bowl. Pour the spice mixture over the beef ribs and rub the spices into the meat. Place the ribs in the slow cooker and add water. Then add the chopped tomato and garlic clove. Close the lid and cook the beef ribs for 5 hours on Low. Cool the ribs until room temperature and serve!

Nutrition: calories 182, fat 8.2, fiber 1.1, carbs 4.1, protein 22.1

Bacon Meatloaf

Prep time: 15 minutes | Cooking time: 3 hours | Servings: 6

Ingredients:
- 10 oz ground chicken
- 5 oz bacon, sliced
- 1 tablespoon butter
- 1 egg yolk
- 1 teaspoon salt
- 1 teaspoon chili pepper
- ½ teaspoon cayenne pepper
- 1 teaspoon ground black pepper
- 1 teaspoon olive oil
- 1 garlic clove, diced

Directions:
Mix the ground chicken, egg yolk, butter, chili pepper, cayenne pepper, ground black pepper, and diced garlic. Stir the mixture and then place it in the slow cooker. Cover the groundchicken mixture with the sliced bacon and close the lid. Cook the meatloaf for 3 hours on High. Cool the cooked meatloaf and transfer it to a serving platter. Slice it and

Nutrition: calories 253, fat 16.9, fiber 0.2, carbs 1, protein 23

Keto Pork Tenderloin

Prep time: 15 minutes | Cooking time: 3 hours | Servings: 2

Ingredients:
- 9 oz pork tenderloin
- ½ teaspoon ground black pepper
- 2 tablespoons butter
- 2 garlic clove, peeled
- ½ teaspoon salt
- ¼ cup water

Directions:
Sprinkle the pork tenderloins with the ground black pepper and salt. Place the pork tenderloin in the slow cooker. Add the peeled garlic and water. Add the butter and close the lid. Cook the pork tenderloins for 3 hours on High. When the time is done and the meat is cooked, let it cool slightly.

Nutrition: calories 290, fat 16, fiber 0.2, carbs 1.3, protein 33.8

Lamb Stew

Prep time: 15 minutes | Cooking time: 60 minutes | Servings: 6

Ingredients:
- 1 onion, chopped
- 5 oz broccoli, chopped
- 4 oz eggplant, chopped
- 1 garlic clove, peeled
- 1 cup water
- 1 zucchini, chopped
- 8 oz lamb fillet, chopped
- 1 teaspoon cayenne pepper
- 1 teaspoon salt

Directions:
Place the chopped onion, broccoli, and eggplant in the slow cooker. Add water and chopped zucchini. Dice the garlic clove and add it to the slow cooker too. Add chopped lamb fillet, salt, and cayenne pepper. Stir the stew gently. Close the lid and cook the lamb stew for 7 hours on Low. Serve the lamb stew hot.

Nutrition: calories 97, fat 3, fiber 2.1, carbs 5.8, protein 12.1

Delicious Turmeric Beef Stew

Prep time: 15 minutes | Cooking time: 5 hours | Servings: 4

Ingredients:
- 7 oz ground beef
- 1 tablespoon turmeric
- 1 onion, diced
- 7 oz broccoli
- 1 cup water
- 1 tablespoon full-fat cream
- 1 teaspoon salt
- ½ teaspoon cayenne pepper

Directions:
Mix the ground beef and turmeric. Add the diced onion, salt, and cayenne pepper. Stir the ingredients and transfer into the slow cooker. Add the broccoli and water. Add the full-fat cream and stir the stew gently. Close the lid and cook the stew for 5 hours on Low. Chill the cooked stew slightly and serve!

Nutrition: calories 132, fat 3.9, fiber 2.3, carbs 7.3, protein 17

Asian Chopped Beef

Prep time: 20 minutes | Cooking time: 3 hours | Servings: 4

Ingredients:
- 1-pound beef chops
- 2 tablespoons apple cider vinegar
- 1 tablespoon dried mint
- 1 tablespoon olive oil
- 1 teaspoon mustard
- ¼ teaspoon salt
- ¼ cup water

Directions:
Chop the beef roughly and sprinkle it with the apple cider vinegar, dried mint, mustard, olive oil, and salt. Stir the meat and let it sit for 20 minutes to marinate. Transfer the meat to the slow cooker and add water. Cook the beef for 3 hours on High. When the beef is cooked, let it rest for 10 minutes and serve!

Nutrition: calories 187, fat 8.8, fiber 0.2, carbs 2.6, protein 23.2

Spicy Bacon Strips

Prep time: 15 minutes | Cooking time: 2 hours | Servings: 4

Ingredients:
- 1 teaspoon cayenne pepper
- ½ teaspoon ground red pepper
- 1 tablespoon olive oil
- ¼ teaspoon ground black pepper
- 7 oz bacon, sliced
- 1 onion, sliced
- 1 teaspoon butter

Directions:
Cut the bacon into the strips. Sprinkle the bacon strips with the ground red pepper, ground black pepper, and olive oil. Place the bacon strips in the slow cooker and add sliced onion and butter. Close the lid and cook the bacon for 2 hours on High. Stir the bacon and transfer on to serving plates.

Nutrition: calories 320, fat 25.3, fiber 0.7, carbs 3.6, protein 18.8

Paprika Pork Sausages

Prep time: 15 minutes | Cooking time: 2 hours | Servings: 4

Ingredients:
- 10 oz ground pork
- 1 tablespoon paprika
- 2 egg yolks
- ½ teaspoon salt
- 1 teaspoon ground black pepper
- ½ onion, grated
- 1 tablespoon almond flour

Directions:
Mix the ground pork and egg yolks. Stir the ground pork with a fork until well blended. Add paprika, salt, ground black pepper, and almond flour. Stir the pork mixture and add the grated onion. Stir it well and form medium sausages using your hands. Then place the sausages in the slow cooker. Close the lid and cook for 2 hours on High. Then transfer the sausages to the platter and

Nutrition: calories 180, fat 8.5, fiber 1.8, carbs 4.4, protein 21.9

Chicken Stew

Prep time: 35 minutes | Cooking time: 5 hours | Servings: 6

Ingredients:
- 8 oz cauliflower, chopped
- 1 zucchini, chopped
- 1 cup water
- 8 oz chicken thighs
- ½ teaspoon salt
- ½ teaspoon paprika
- 1 teaspoon cayenne pepper
- 1 tablespoon butter
- 1 onion, sliced
- 1 tomato, chopped

Directions:
Place the chopped cauliflower, zucchini, water, salt, paprika, cayenne pepper, sliced onion, and chopped tomato in the slow cooker. Add butter and chicken thighs. Stir the ingredients gently and close the slow cooker lid. Cook the stew for 5 hours on Low. Leave the stew for 20 minutes to rest. Serve the chicken stew and

Nutrition: calories 114, fat 14.9, fiber 2, carbs 5.5, protein 12.5

Pulled Pork Salad
Prep time: 15 minutes | Cooking time: 8 hours | Servings: 4

Ingredients:
- 1 avocado, chopped
- 1 tomato, chopped
- 1 cup lettuce, chopped
- 1 tablespoon olive oil
- ½ teaspoon chili flakes
- 7 oz pork loin
- 1 cup water
- 1 bay leaf
- 1 teaspoon salt
- ¼ teaspoon peppercorns

Directions:
Place the pork loin in the slow cooker. Add the water, bay leaf, salt, and peppercorns. Add the chili flakes and close the lid. Cook the pork loin for 8 hours on Low. Meanwhile, mix the chopped avocado, tomato, and lettuce in a large salad bowl. When the pork loin is cooked, remove it from the water and place it in a separate bowl. Shred the pork loin with two forks. Add the shredded pork loin into the salad bowl. Stir the salad gently and sprinkle with the olive oil.

Nutrition: calories 258, fat 20.3, fiber 3.8, carbs 5.6, protein 14.7

Garlic Pork Belly
Prep time: 15 minutes | Cooking time: 7 hours | Servings: 8

Ingredients:
- 1-pound pork belly
- 4 garlic cloves, peeled
- 1 teaspoon peppercorns
- 2 tablespoons mustard
- ½ teaspoon salt
- 1 tablespoon butter
- 1 cup water

Directions:
Dice the garlic cloves and combine them with the peppercorns and mustard. Add the salt and butter and stir. Rub the pork belly with the prepared mixture well. Place the pork belly in the slow cooker. Add the water and close the lid. Cook the pork belly for 7 hours on Low. Slice the cooked pork belly and serve!

Nutrition: calories 290, fat 17.5, fiber 0.5, carbs 1.7, protein 27

Sesame Seed Shrimp
Prep time: 20 minutes | Cooking time: 30 minutes | Servings: 4

Ingredients:
- 1-pound shrimp, peeled
- 2 tablespoons apple cider vinegar
- 1 teaspoon paprika
- 1 teaspoon sesame seeds
- ¼ cup water
- 3 tablespoons butter

Directions:
Sprinkle the shrimp with the apple cider vinegar. Add paprika and stir the shrimp. Let the shrimp marinade for 15 minutes. Pour water into the slow cooker. Add the butter and marinated shrimp. Cook the shrimp for 30 minutes on High. Transfer the shrimp to a serving bowl. Mix together the remainingliquid and sesame seeds. Sprinkle the shrimp with the sesame mixture and

Nutrition: calories 219, fat 11, fiber 0.3, carbs 2.3, protein 26.1

Cod Fillet in Coconut Flakes

Prep time: 20 minutes | Cooking time: 1 hour | Servings: 4

Ingredients:
- ¼ cup coconut flakes, unsweetened
- 1 egg, beaten
- ½ teaspoon salt
- 1 teaspoon ground black pepper
- 10 oz cod fillets
- 1 tablespoon butter
- 3 tablespoons water

Directions:
Whisk the egg, combine it with the salt, and ground black pepper. Place the cod fillets in the egg mixture and stir well. Coat the egged cod fillets in the coconut flakes. Add the butter to the slow cooker. Add water and coated cod fillets. Close the lid and cook the fish for 1 hour on High. Then transfer the cod fillets onto a cutting board and cut them into servings. the cod fillet warm!

Nutrition: calories 117, fat 6.3, fiber 0.6, carbs 1.2, protein 14.3

Chicken Liver Pate

Prep time: 25 minutes | Cooking time: 2 hours | Servings: 6

Ingredients:
- 1-pound chicken liver
- 1 onion, chopped
- 2 cups water
- 1 teaspoon salt
- ¼ teaspoon ground nutmeg
- 2 tablespoons butter
- 1 bay leaf

Directions:
Place the chicken liver in the slow cooker. Add chopped onion, water, salt, ground black pepper, and bay leaf. Close the lid and cook the liver for 2 hours on High. After this, strain the chicken liver, discarding the liquid, and place it in the blender. Add butter and blend the mixture until smooth (approximately for 3 minutes at maximum speed). Transfer the cooked pate into a bowl and let it cool in the freezer for 10 minutes. Serve with keto bread!

Nutrition: calories 168, fat 8.8, fiber 0.5, carbs 2.5, protein 18.8

Garlic Duck Breast

Prep time: 20 minutes | Cooking time: 5 hours | Servings: 6

Ingredients:
- 11 oz duck breast, boneless, skinless
- 4 garlic cloves, roughly diced
- 1 teaspoon rosemary
- 1 tablespoon butter
- ½ cup water
- 1 teaspoon chili flakes

Directions:
Make small cuts in the duck breast. Sprinkle the duck breast with the rosemary and chili flakes. Fill the cuts with the diced garlic. Place the duck breast in the slow cooker. Add butter and water and close the lid. Cook the duck breast for 5 hours on Low. When the duck breast is cooked, remove it from the slow cooker and let it rest for 10 minutes. Slice the duck breast and serve!

Nutrition: calories 88, fat 4, fiber 0.1, carbs 0.8, protein 11.6

Thyme Lamb Chops

Prep time: 20 minutes | Cooking time: 7 hours | Servings: 2

Ingredients:
- 8 oz lamb chops
- 1 teaspoon liquid stevia
- 1 teaspoon thyme
- 1 tablespoon olive oil
- ¼ cup water
- 1 bay leaf
- ¾ teaspoon ground cinnamon
- ½ onion, chopped

Directions:
Mix the liquid stevia, thyme, olive oil, and ground cinnamon. Rub the lamb chops with the spice mixture. Place the lamb chops in the slow cooker and add chopped onion and water. Add the bay leaf and close the lid. Cook the lamb chops for 7 hours on Low. When the meat is cooked, serve it immediately!

Nutrition: calories 287, fat 15.4, fiber 1.4, carbs 4, protein 32.3

Autumn Pork Stew

Prep time: 30 minutes | Cooking time: 6 hours | Servings: 5

Ingredients:
- 1 eggplant, chopped
- 4 oz white mushrooms, chopped
- 1 white onion, chopped
- 2 cups water
- ½ teaspoon clove
- ½ teaspoon salt
- ½ teaspoon cayenne pepper
- 8 oz pork tenderloin

Directions:
Place the chopped eggplant, mushrooms, onion, and water in the slow cooker. Chop the pork tenderloin roughly and sprinkle it with the cayenne pepper, salt, and clove. Stir the meat and place it in the slow cooker too. Close the lid and cook the stew for 6 hours on Low. When the stew is cooked, let it rest for 20 minutes.

Nutrition: calories 232, fat 5.1, fiber 4.1, carbs 8.4, protein 37.5

Handmade Sausage Stew

Prep time: 25 minutes | Cooking time: 3 hours | Servings: 3

Ingredients:
- 7 oz ground pork
- 1 egg yolk
- ½ teaspoon salt
- ½ teaspoon ground black pepper
- 7 oz broccoli, chopped
- ½ cup water
- 1 tomato, chopped
- 1 teaspoon butter

Directions:
Mix the ground pork and yolk. Add salt and ground black pepper. Stir the mixture and form small sausages with your hands. Place the sausages in the slow cooker. Add the chopped broccoli and water. Add chopped tomato and butter. Close the lid and cook the stew for 3 hours on High. Place the cooked stew in bowls and

Nutrition: calories 151, fat 5.4, fiber 2.1, carbs 5.6, protein 20.3

Marinated Beef Tenderloin

Prep time: 20 minutes | Cooking time: 6 hours | Servings: 6

Ingredients:
- 2 tablespoons butter
- 1-pound Beef Tenderloin
- 1 teaspoon minced garlic
- ½ teaspoon ground nutmeg
- 1 teaspoon turmeric
- 1 teaspoon paprika
- 1 tablespoon apple cider vinegar
- ½ teaspoon dried oregano
- 1 cup water

Directions:
Melt the butter and mix it up with the minced garlic, ground nutmeg, turmeric, paprika, apple cider vinegar, and dried oregano. Whisk the mixture. Rub the beef tenderloin with the spice mixture. Place the beef tenderloin in the slow cooker and add the remaining spice mixture. Add water and close the lid. Cook the beef tenderloin for 8 hours on Low. Chop the beef tenderloin and serve it!

Nutrition: calories 208, fat 6, fiber .5, carbs 3, protein 24

Chicken Liver Sauté

Prep time: 20 minutes | Cooking time: 5 hours | Servings: 4

Ingredients:
- 10 oz chicken liver
- 1 onion, chopped
- 2 tablespoons full-fat cream
- 5 oz white mushrooms, chopped
- 1 cup water
- 1 tablespoon butter
- 1 teaspoon salt
- ½ teaspoon ground black pepper

Directions:
Placethechicken liver, onion, full-fat cream, mushrooms, water, butter, salt, and ground black pepper in the slow cooker and close the lid. Cook the mixture for 5 hours on Low. When the liver saute is cooked, let it rest for 10 minutes.

Nutrition: calories 245, fat 11.4, fiber 0.5, carbs 1.4, protein 32.6

Chicken in Bacon

Prep time: 20 minutes | Cooking time: 3 hours | Servings: 6

Ingredients:
- 1-pound chicken thighs
- 7 oz bacon, sliced
- 1 tablespoon butter
- ¾ cup water
- ½ teaspoon ground black pepper
- 1 teaspoon chili flakes
- 1 teaspoon paprika

Directions:
Sprinkle the chicken thighs with the ground black pepper, chili flakes, and paprika. Wrap the chicken thighs in the sliced bacon and transfer to the slow cooker. Add the water and butter and close the lid. Cook the chicken for 3 hours on High. Serve the cooked meal immediately!

Nutrition: calories 341, fat 21.4, fiber 0.2, carbs 0.8, protein 34.2

Whole Chicken

Prep time: 40 minutes | Cooking time: 10 hours | Servings: 10

Ingredients:
- 2-pound whole chicken
- 4 oz celery stalk, chopped
- 1 onion, chopped
- 3 garlic cloves, peeled
- 1 tablespoon rosemary
- 1 teaspoon dried oregano
- 2 tablespoons butter
- 1 teaspoon salt
- ½ teaspoon ground coriander
- 1 teaspoon turmeric
- 2 cups water

Directions:
Rub the chicken with the rosemary, dried oregano, salt, ground coriander, and turmeric. Fill the chicken cavity with the chopped celery, garlic cloves, onion, and butter. Place the chicken in the slow cooker and add water. Close the lid and cook the chicken for 10 hours on Low. When the chicken is cooked, leave it for 20 minutes to rest. Serve and

Nutrition: calories 203, fat 9.1, fiber 0.7, carbs 2.1, protein 26.6

Duck Rolls

Prep time: 25 minutes | Cooking time: 3 hours | Servings: 6

Ingredients:
- 2-pound duck fillets
- 1 teaspoon minced garlic
- 1 cup spinach, chopped
- ¼ cup water
- 1 teaspoon rosemary
- 1 tablespoon olive oil

Directions:
Beat the duck fillets gently to tenderize and flatten then sprinkle them with the minced garlic, rosemary, and olive oil. Place the chopped spinach on each of the duck fillets and roll them up, enclosing the spinach inside the duck. Secure the duck rolls with the toothpicks and place them in the slow cooker. Add water and close the lid. Cook the duck rolls for 3 hours on High. Cool the rolls slightly and serve!

Nutrition: calories 210, fat 3.3, fiber 0.2, carbs 0.5, protein 44.8

Keto Adobo Chicken

Prep time: 15 minutes | Cooking time: 2 hours | Servings: 4

Ingredients:
- 1-pound chicken breast, boneless, skinless
- 1 tablespoon soy sauce
- 1 tablespoon olive oil
- 1 tablespoon apple cider vinegar
- 1 teaspoon minced garlic

Directions:
Chop the chicken breast roughly and sprinkle it with the soy sauce, olive oil, apple cider vinegar, and minced garlic. Mix and then let sit for 20 minutes to marinate. Transfer the chicken and all the remaining liquid into the slow cooker. Close the lid and cook the meal for 2 hours on High.

Nutrition: calories 163, fat 6.3, fiber 0, carbs 0.6, protein 24.3

Cayenne Pepper Drumsticks

Prep time: 20 minutes | Cooking time: 5 hours | Servings: 2

Ingredients:
- 10 oz chicken drumsticks
- 1 teaspoon cayenne pepper
- 1 bell pepper, chopped
- ½ cup water
- 1 tablespoon butter
- 1 teaspoon thyme
- 1 teaspoon cumin
- ½ teaspoon chili pepper

Directions:
Mix the cayenne pepper, chopped bell pepper, butter, thyme, cumin, and chili pepper. Stir the mixture until smooth, Rub the chicken drumsticks with the spice mixture and place them in the slow cooker. Add water and close the lid. Cook the drumsticks for 5 hours on Low. Transfer the cooked meal onto a platter and serve!

Nutrition: calories 318, fat 14.4, fiber 1.4, carbs 5.9, protein 40

Keto BBQ Chicken Wings

Prep time: 20 minutes | Cooking time: 2 hours | Servings: 4

Ingredients:
- 1-pound chicken wings
- 1 teaspoon minced garlic
- 1 teaspoon cumin
- 1 teaspoon ground coriander
- 1 teaspoon dried dill
- 1 teaspoon dried parsley
- 1 tablespoon mustard
- 1 teaspoon liquid stevia
- 1 tablespoon tomato paste
- 1 teaspoon salt
- 1 tablespoon apple cider vinegar

Directions:
Mix the minced garlic, cumin, ground coriander, dried dill, dried parsley, mustard, liquid stevia, tomato paste, salt, and apple cider vinegar. Stir the mixture until smooth. Combine the spice mixture and chicken wings and stir well. Transfer the chicken wings and all the remaining spice mixture into the slow cooker. Close the lid and cook for 2 hours on High. Cool the chicken wings slightly and serve!

Nutrition: calories 236, fat 9.4, fiber 0.7, carbs 2.4, protein 33.9

Prawn Stew

Prep time: 15 minutes | Cooking time: 1 hour | Servings: 4

Ingredients:
- 10 oz prawns, peeled
- 1 onion, sliced
- 4 oz Parmesan, grated
- 1 garlic clove, peeled
- 1 teaspoon salt
- ½ cup almond milk
- 1 teaspoon butter
- 1 teaspoon chili flakes

Directions:
Place the peeled prawns, sliced onion, garlic clove, salt, almond milk, butter, and chili flakes into the slow cooker. Close the lid and cook the stew for 1 hour on High. Transfer the cooked stew into serving bowls and sprinkle with the grated cheese. Serve it!

Nutrition: calories 265, fat 15.4, fiber 1.3, carbs 6.6, protein 26.3

Pork-Jalapeno Bowl

Prep time: 15 minutes | Cooking time: 3 hours | Servings: 4

Ingredients:
- 2 jalapeno peppers, chopped
- 9 oz pork chops
- 1 onion, grated
- ½ cup water
- 1 teaspoon butter
- ½ teaspoon chili flakes
- 1 teaspoon ground black pepper

Directions:
Sprinkle the pork chops with the chili flakes and ground black pepper. Place the pork chops in the slow cooker. Add water, grated onion, and butter, Add the jalapeno peppers and close the lid. Cook the meal for 3 hours on High. Stir the cooked meal and transfer it to serving bowls. Serve it!

Nutrition: calories 228, fat 17, fiber 1, carbs 3.4, protein 14.8

Chicken Marsala

Prep time: 15 minutes | Cooking time: 7 hours | Servings: 4

Ingredients:
- 1-pound chicken breast, skinless, boneless
- 2 oz white mushrooms, chopped
- 1 oz Marsala cooking wine
- 1 teaspoon garlic powder
- 3 tablespoons butter
- 1 teaspoon salt
- 1 teaspoon ground black pepper

Directions:
Chop the chicken breast roughly and sprinkle it with the garlic powder, salt, and ground black pepper. Stir the chicken and transfer it to the slow cooker. Add butter, Marsala cooking wine, mushrooms, and close the lid. Cook chicken Marsala for 7 hours on Low. Stir the cooked meal gently. Serve it in serving bowls.

Nutrition: calories 219, fat 11.6, fiber 0.4, carbs 2.3, protein 24.8

Side Dishes

Zucchini Pasta

Prep time: 15 minutes | Cooking time: 1 hour | Servings: 4

Ingredients:
- 2 zucchini
- 1 teaspoon dried oregano
- 1 teaspoon dried basil
- 2 tablespoons butter
- ¼ teaspoon salt
- 5 tablespoons water

Directions:
Peel the zucchini and spiralize it with a veggie spiralizer. Melt the butter and mix it together with the dried oregano, dried basil, salt, and water. Place the spiralized zucchini in the slow cooker and add the spice mixture. Close the lid and cook the meal for 1 hour on Low. Let the cooked pasta cool slightly. Serve it!

Nutrition: calories 68, fat 6, fiber 1.2, carbs 3.5, protein 1.3

Chinese Broccoli

Prep time: 15 minutes | Cooking time: 1 hour | Servings: 4

Ingredients:
- 1 tablespoon sesame seeds
- 1 tablespoon olive oil
- 10 oz broccoli
- 1 teaspoon chili flakes
- 1 tablespoon apple cider vinegar
- 3 tablespoons water
- ¼ teaspoon garlic powder

Directions:
Cut the broccoli into the florets and sprinkle with the olive oil, chili flakes, apple cider vinegar, and garlic powder. Stir the broccoli and place it in the slow cooker. Add water and sesame seeds. Cook the broccoli for 1 hour on High. Transfer the cooked broccolito serving plates and

Nutrition: calories 69, fat 4.9, fiber 2.1, carbs 5.4, protein 2.4

Slow Cooker Spaghetti Squash

Prep time: 15 minutes | Cooking time: 4 hours | Servings: 5

Ingredients:
- 1-pound spaghetti squash
- 1 tablespoon butter
- ¼ cup water
- 1 teaspoon ground black pepper
- ¼ teaspoon ground nutmeg

Directions:
Peel the spaghetti squash and sprinkle it with the ground black pepper and ground nutmeg. Pour water in the slow cooker. Add butter and spaghetti squash. Close the lid and cook for 4 hours on Low. Chop the spaghetti squash into small pieces and serve!

Nutrition: calories 50, fat 2.9, fiber 6.6, carbs 0.1, protein 0.7

Mushroom Stew

Prep time: 15 minutes | Cooking time: 6 hours | Servings: 8

Ingredients:
- 10 oz white mushrooms, sliced
- 2 eggplants, chopped
- 1 onion, diced
- 1 garlic clove, diced
- 2 bell peppers, chopped
- 1 cup water
- 1 tablespoon butter
- ½ teaspoon salt
- ½ teaspoon ground black pepper

Directions:
Place the sliced mushrooms, chopped eggplant, and diced onion into the slow cooker. Add garlic clove and bell peppers. Sprinkle the vegetables with salt and ground black pepper. Add butter and water and stir it gently with a wooden spatula. Close the lid and cook the stew for 6 hours on Low. Stir the cooked stew one more time and serve!

Nutrition: calories 71, fat 1.9, fiber 5.9, carbs 13, protein 3

Cabbage Steaks

Prep time: 15 minutes | Cooking time: 2 hours | Servings: 4

Ingredients:
- 10 oz white cabbage
- 1 tablespoon butter
- ½ teaspoon cayenne pepper
- ½ teaspoon chili flakes
- 4 tablespoons water

Directions:
Slice the cabbage into medium steaks and rub them with the cayenne pepper and chili flakes. Rub the cabbage steaks with butter on each side. Place them in the slow cooker and sprinkle with water. Close the lid and cook the cabbage steaks for 2 hours on High. When the cabbage steaks are cooked, they should be tender to the touch. Serve the cabbage steak after 10 minutes of chilling.

Nutrition: calories 44, fat 3, fiber 1.8, carbs 4.3, protein 1

Mashed Cauliflower

Prep time: 20 minutes | Cooking time: 3 hours | Servings: 5

Ingredients:
- 3 tablespoons butter
- 1-pound cauliflower
- 1 tablespoons full-fat cream
- 1 teaspoon salt
- 1 teaspoon ground black pepper
- 1 oz dill, chopped

Directions:
Wash the cauliflower and chop it. Place the chopped cauliflower in the slow cooker. Add butter and full-fat cream. Add salt and ground black pepper. Stir the mixture and close the lid. Cook the cauliflower for 3 hours on High. When the cauliflower is cooked, transfer it to a blender and blend until smooth. Place the smooth cauliflower in a bowl and mix with the chopped dill. Stir it well and serve!

Nutrition: calories 101, fat 7.4, fiber 3.2, carbs 8.3, protein 3.1

Bacon Wrapped Cauliflower

Prep time: 15 minutes | Cooking time: 7 hours | Servings: 4

Ingredients:
- 11 oz cauliflower head
- 3 oz bacon, sliced
- 1 teaspoon salt
- 1 teaspoon cayenne pepper
- 1 oz butter, softened
- ¾ cup water

Directions:
Sprinkle the cauliflower head with the salt and cayenne pepper then rub with butter. Wrap the cauliflower head in the sliced bacon and secure with toothpicks. Pour water in the slow cooker and add the wrapped cauliflower head. Cook the cauliflower head for 7 hours on Low. Then let the cooked cauliflower head cool for 10 minutes. Serve it!

Nutrition: calories 187, fat 14.8, fiber 2.1, carbs 4.7, protein 9.5

Cauliflower Casserole

Prep time: 15 minutes | Cooking time: 7 hours | Servings: 5

Ingredients:
- 2 tomatoes, chopped
- 11 oz cauliflower chopped
- 5 oz broccoli, chopped
- 1 cup water
- 1 teaspoon salt
- 1 tablespoon butter
- 5 oz white mushrooms, chopped
- 1 teaspoon chili flakes

Directions:
Mix the water, salt, and chili flakes. Place the butter in the slow cooker. Add a layer of the chopped cauliflower. Add the layer of broccoli and tomatoes. Add the mushrooms and pat down the mix to flatten. Add the water and close the lid. Cook the casserole for 7 hours on Low. Cool the casserole to room temperature and serve!

Nutrition: calories 61, fat 2.6, fiber 3.2, carbs 8.1, protein 3.4

Cauliflower Rice

Prep time: 15 minutes | Cooking time: 2 hours | Servings: 5

Ingredients:
- 1-pound cauliflower
- 1 teaspoon salt
- 1 tablespoon turmeric
- 1 tablespoon butter
- ¾ cup water

Directions:
Chop the cauliflower into tiny pieces to make cauliflower rice. You can also pulse in a food processor to get very fine grains of 'rice'. Place the cauliflower rice in the slow cooker. Add salt, turmeric, and water. Stir gently and close the lid. Cook the cauliflower rice for 2 hours on High. Strain the cauliflower rice and transfer it toa bowl. Add butter and stir gently. Serve it!

Nutrition: calories 48, fat 2.5, fiber 2.6, carbs 5.7, protein 1.9

Curry Cauliflower

Prep time: 15 minutes | Cooking time: 5 hours | Servings: 2

Ingredients:
- 10 oz cauliflower
- 1 teaspoon curry paste
- 1 teaspoon curry powder
- ½ teaspoon dried cilantro
- 1 oz butter
- ¾ cup water
- ¼ cup chicken stock

Directions:
Chop the cauliflower roughly and sprinkle it with the curry powder and dried cilantro. Place the chopped cauliflower in the slow cooker. Mix the curry paste with the water. Add chicken stock and transfer the liquid to the slow cooker. Add butter and close the lid. Cook the cauliflower for 5 hours on Low. Strain ½ of the liquid off and discard. Transfer the cauliflower to serving bowls. Serve it!

Nutrition: calories 158, fat 13.3, fiber 3.9, carbs 8.9, protein 3.3

Garlic Cauliflower Steaks

Prep time: 15 minutes | Cooking time: 3 hours | Servings: 4

Ingredients:
- 14 oz cauliflower head
- 1 teaspoon minced garlic
- 4 tablespoons butter
- 4 tablespoons water
- 1 teaspoon paprika

Directions:
Wash the cauliflower head carefully and slice it into the medium steaks. Mix up together the butter, minced garlic, and paprika. Rub the cauliflower steaks with the butter mixture. Pour the water in the slow cooker. Add the cauliflower steaks and close the lid. Cook the vegetables for 3 hours on High. Transfer the cooked cauliflower steaks to a platter and serve them immediately!

Nutrition: calories 129, fat 11.7, fiber 2.7, carbs 5.8, protein 2.2

Zucchini Gratin

Prep time: 10 minutes | Cooking time: 5 hours | Servings: 3

Ingredients:
- 1 zucchini, sliced
- 3 oz Parmesan, grated
- 1 teaspoon ground black pepper
- 1 tablespoon butter
- ½ cup almond milk

Directions:
Sprinkle the sliced zucchini with the ground black pepper. Chop the butter and place it in the slow cooker. Transfer the sliced zucchini to the slow cooker to make the bottom layer. Add the almond milk. Sprinkle the zucchini with the grated cheese and close the lid. Cook the gratin for 5 hours on Low. Then let the gratin cool until room temperature. Serve it!

Nutrition: calories 229, fat 19.6, fiber 1.8, carbs 5.9, protein 10.9

Eggplant Gratin

Prep time: 15 minutes | Cooking time: 5 hours | Servings: 7

Ingredients:
- 1 tablespoon butter
- 1 teaspoon minced garlic
- 2 eggplants, chopped
- 1 teaspoon salt
- 1 tablespoon dried parsley
- 4 oz Parmesan, grated
- 4 tablespoons water
- 1 teaspoon chili flakes

Directions:
Mix the dried parsley, chili flakes, and salt together. Sprinkle the chopped eggplants with the spice mixture and stir well. Place the eggplants in the slow cooker. Add the water and minced garlic. Add the butter and sprinkle with the grated Parmesan. Close the lid and cook the gratin for 5 hours on Low. Open the lid and cool the gratin for 10 minutes. Serve it.

Nutrition: calories 107, fat 5.4, fiber 5.6, carbs 10, protein 6.8

Moroccan Eggplant Mash

Prep time: 15 minutes | Cooking time: 7 hours | Servings: 4

Ingredients:
- 1 eggplant, peeled
- 1 jalapeno pepper
- 1 teaspoon curry powder
- ½ teaspoon salt
- 1 teaspoon paprika
- ¾ teaspoon ground nutmeg
- 2 tablespoons butter
- ¾ cup almond milk
- 1 teaspoon dried dill

Directions:
Chop the eggplant into small pieces. Place the eggplant in the slow cooker. Chop the jalapeno pepper and combine it with the eggplant. Then sprinkle the vegetables with the curry powder, salt, paprika, ground nutmeg, and dried dill. Add almond milk and butter. Close the lid and cook the vegetables for 7 hours on Low. Cool the vegetables and then blend them until smooth with a hand blender. Transfer the cooked eggplant mash into the bowls and serve!

Nutrition: calories 190, fat 17, fiber 5.6, carbs 10, protein 2.5

Sautéed Bell Peppers

Prep time: 15 minutes | Cooking time: 5 hours | Servings: 6

Ingredients:
- 8 oz bell peppers
- 7 oz cauliflower, chopped
- 2 oz bacon, chopped
- 1 teaspoon salt
- 1 teaspoon ground black pepper
- ¾ cup coconut milk, unsweetened
- 1 teaspoon butter
- 1 teaspoon thyme
- 1 onion, diced
- 1 teaspoon turmeric

Directions:
Remove the seeds from the bell peppers and chop them roughly. Place the bell peppers, cauliflower, and bacon in the slow cooker. Add the salt, ground black pepper, coconut milk, butter, milk, and thyme. Stir well then add the diced onion. Add the turmeric and stir the mixture. Close the lid and cook 5 hours on Low. When the meal is cooked, let it chill for 10 minutes and serve it!

Nutrition: calories 195, fat 12.2, fiber 4.2, carbs 13.1, protein 6.7

Garlic Artichoke

Prep time: 15 minutes | Cooking time: 2 hours | Servings: 4

Ingredients:
- 8 oz artichoke, trimmed, chopped
- 2 teaspoons butter
- 1 garlic clove, peeled
- ¼ cup water
- ½ tea spoon ground black pepper

Directions:
Chop the garlic clove. Melt the butter and mix it with the chopped garlic. Add the ground black pepper and stir the mixture. Place the artichoke in the slow cooker and cover it with the butter mixture. Add water and close the lid. Cook the artichoke for 2 hours on High. Transfer the cooked artichoke to a platter and serve!

Nutrition: calories 45, fat 2, fiber 3.2, carbs 6.4, protein 2

Broccoli Stew

Prep time: 15 minutes | Cooking time: 6 hours | Servings: 3

Ingredients:
- 6 oz broccoli, chopped
- 1 cup spinach
- ¾ cup almond milk, unsweetened
- 2 oz white cabbage, shredded
- 1 tablespoon butter
- 1 teaspoon salt
- 1 teaspoon white pepper
- 2 cups water

Directions:
Chop the spinach and place it in the slow cooker. Add chopped broccoli, almond milk, shredded cabbage, butter, salt, water and white pepper. Stir the ingredients and close the lid. Cook the stew for 6 hours on Low. Stir the stew gently and transfer to serving bowls.

Nutrition: calories 200, fat 18.4, fiber 3.7, carbs 9, protein 3.6

Spiced Fennel Slices

Prep time: 15 minutes | Cooking time: 2 hours | Servings: 5

Ingredients:
- 1-pound fennel bulb
- 1 teaspoon cumin
- 1 teaspoon thyme
- 1 teaspoon salt
- 1 oz butter
- 1 tablespoon olive oil

Directions:

Mix the cumin, thyme, salt, and olive oil. Slice the fennel bulb and sprinkle it with the spice mixture. Place the fennel in the slow cooker and add butter. Close the lid and cook for 2 hours on High. Serve the meal hot!

Nutrition: calories 95, fat 7.7, fiber 2.9, carbs 6.9, protein 1.3

Okra Stew

Prep time: 15 minutes | Cooking time: 5 hours | Servings: 4

Ingredients:
- 10 oz okra, chopped
- 1 onion, diced
- 5 oz cauliflower, chopped
- 1 cup water
- 1 teaspoon butter
- 1 teaspoon paprika
- ½ teaspoon ground black pepper
- 1 teaspoon dried dill

Directions:

Mix the chopped okra, dicedonion, cauliflower, and spices. Stir the mixture and place it in the slow cooker. Add water and butter and close the lid. Cook the stew for 5 hours on Low. Transfer the dish into serving bowls and serve!

Nutrition: calories 59, fat 1.3, fiber 4.1, carbs 10.3, protein 2.5

Sesame Snow Peas

Prep time: 10 minutes | Cooking time: 1 hour | Servings: 4

Ingredients:
- 1-pound snow peas
- 1 tablespoon sesame seeds
- 1 teaspoon cayenne pepper
- 1 teaspoon butter
- 1 cup water

Directions:

Place the snow peas in the slow cooker. Add the cayenne pepper, sesame seeds, and butter. Add water and close the lid. Cook the snow peas for 1 hour on High. Strain the vegetables and serve them immediately!

Nutrition: calories 70, fat 2.4, fiber 3.6, carbs 8.8, protein 4.2

Coconut Kale

Prep time: 10 minutes | Cooking time: 30 minutes | Servings: 6

Ingredients:
- 10 oz Italian dark-leaf kale
- 1 tablespoon coconut flakes, unsweetened
- ½ cup coconut milk, unsweetened
- 1 teaspoon almonds, crushed
- 1 teaspoon butter
- ½ teaspoon turmeric

Directions:
Chop the kale and place it in the slow cooker. Add the coconut milk, butter, and turmeric. Close the lid and cook the kale for 30 minutes on High. Transfer the kale to serving plates. Sprinkle with the crushed almonds and coconut flakes. Serve it!

Nutrition: calories 80, fat 5.9, fiber 1.3, carbs 6.4, protein 2

Tomato Gratin with Bell Pepper

Prep time: 15 minutes | Cooking time: 4 hours | Servings: 4

Ingredients:
- 2 tomatoes, sliced
- 6 oz bell pepper, sliced
- 4 oz Parmesan, grated
- ¼ cup almond milk, unsweetened
- 1 tablespoons dried parsley
- ¼ teaspoon ground coriander
- 1 teaspoon butter
- 1 garlic clove, diced

Directions:
Chop the butter and place it in the slow cooker. Make a layer of the sliced tomatoes in the bottom of the slow cooker on top of the butter. Next, make a layer of the bell peppers. Sprinkle the vegetables with the almond milk, dried parsley, ground coriander, and diced garlic clove. Place the grated cheese over the vegetables and close the lid. Cook the gratin for 4 hours on Low. Serve the side dish immediately!

Nutrition: calories 204, fat 1.2, fiber 3.5, carbs 18, protein 11.9

Spicy Mushrooms

Prep time: 15 minutes | Cooking time: 2 hours | Servings: 4

Ingredients:
- 8 oz white mushrooms
- 1 onion, diced
- ¼ cup almond milk, unsweetened
- 1 teaspoon white pepper
- 1 teaspoon ground black pepper
- 1 teaspoon paprika
- 1 teaspoon cayenne pepper
- 1 teaspoon chili flakes

Directions:
Chop the mushrooms roughly. Sprinkle the mushrooms with the white pepper, ground black pepper, paprika, cayenne pepper, and chili flakes. Stir the mushrooms with the spices then place them in the slow cooker. Add the almond milk and diced onion. Cook the mushrooms for 2 hours on High. Let the cooked mushrooms cool slightly. Serve!

Nutrition: calories 62, fat 3.9, fiber 2, carbs 6.2, protein 2.6

Cumin Green Beans

Prep time: 10 minutes | Cooking time: 10 minutes | Servings: 4

Ingredients:
- 8 oz green beans
- 1 teaspoon cumin
- 1 oz butter
- ¾ cup coconut milk, unsweetened
- 1 teaspoon dried cilantro

Directions:
Toss the butter in the slow cooker. Add the coconut milk, cumin and dried cilantro. Stir the liquid with a spatula. Add green beans and close the lid. Cook the side dish for 6 hours on Low. Open the lid and let the beans cool for 10 minutes. Serve it!

Nutrition: calories 174, fat 16.7, fiber 3, carbs 6.8, protein 2.2

Zucchini Fettuccine

Prep time: 15 minutes | Cooking time: 2 hours | Servings: 4

Ingredients:
- 1 zucchini
- 1 tablespoon olive oil
- 1 teaspoon salt
- ½ teaspoon ground black pepper
- 2 tablespoons water

Directions:
Spiralize the zucchini into noodles. Sprinkle 'fettuccine' with the olive oil, salt, and ground black pepper. Transfer the zucchini fettuccine into the slow cooker. Add water and close the lid. Cook the vegies for 2 hours on Low. Serve immediately!

Nutrition: calories 39, fat 3.6, fiber 0.6, carbs 1.8, protein 0.6

Vegetable Stew

Prep time: 25 minutes | Cooking time: 7 hours | Servings: 5

Ingredients:
- 1 cup spinach
- 5 oz white cabbage, chopped
- 5 oz white mushrooms, chopped
- 6 oz cauliflower, chopped
- ½ cup almond milk, unsweetened
- 2 cups water
- 1 garlic clove, peeled
- 1 teaspoon white pepper
- 1 teaspoon chili flakes
- 1 teaspoon turmeric
- 1 teaspoon butter

Directions:
Chop the spinach roughly and place it in the slow cooker. Add white cabbage, mushrooms, and cauliflower. Add almond milk, water, garlic clove, white pepper, chili flakes, and turmeric. Stir the vegetables with a spoon. Add butter and close the lid. Cook the stew for 7 hours on Low. Let the stew cool for 15 minutes. Serve it!

Nutrition: calories 89, fat 6.7, fiber 2.7, carbs 6.7, protein 2.8

Brussel Sprouts with Parmesan

Prep time: 15 minutes | Cooking time: 4 hours 30 minutes | Servings: 3

Ingredients:
- 9 oz Brussel sprouts
- 3 oz Parmesan, sliced
- ¾ cup water
- ¼ teaspoon minced garlic
- 1 teaspoon dried oregano

Directions:
Place Brussel sprouts in the slow cooker. Add the minced garlic and dried oregano. Add the water and cook the vegetables for 4 hours on Low. Strain the Brussel sprouts and place them back in the slow cooker. Add the sliced cheese and cook it for 30 minutes more on High.

Nutrition: calories 130, fat 6.4, fiber 3.4, carbs 9.1, protein 12.1

Garlic Peppers

Prep time: 15 minutes | Cooking time: 4 hours | Servings: 4

Ingredients:
- 4 green peppers
- 1 tablespoon olive oil
- 2 tablespoons water
- 1 teaspoon minced garlic
- 1 teaspoon ground nutmeg
- 1 tablespoon butter

Directions:
Remove the seeds from the green peppers and cut them into the strips. Sprinkle the green peppers with the minced garlic, ground nutmeg, and olive oil. Place the peppers in the slow cooker. Add butter and water. Close the lid and cook on Low for 4 hours. Let the cooked green peppers cool slightly. Serve!

Nutrition: calories 83, fat 6.8, fiber 2.1, carbs 6, protein 1.1

Tender Green Cabbage

Prep time: 15 minutes | Cooking time: 1 hour | Servings: 4

Ingredients:
- ¼ cup almond milk, unsweetened
- 1 oz almonds, chopped
- 11 oz green cabbage, shredded
- 1 teaspoon butter
- 4 tablespoons water

Directions:
Place the shredded green cabbage in the slow cooker. Add butter, water, and almond milk. Stir gently and close the lid. Cook the cabbage for 1 hour on High. Transfer the cooked side dish into the serving bowls. Sprinkle with the chopped almonds and serve!

Nutrition: calories 103, fat 8.2, fiber 3.2, carbs 6.9, protein 2.9

Curled Rutabaga

Prep time: 15 minutes | Cooking time: 2 hours | Servings: 5

Ingredients:
- 13 oz rutabaga
- 1 tablespoon olive oil
- 1 teaspoon ground black pepper
- 1 teaspoon salt
- ½ teaspoon paprika
- 3 tablespoons water

Directions:
Cut the rutabaga into the long strips with the help of the scissors. Sprinkle the rutabaga curls with the olive oil, ground black pepper, salt, and paprika. Stir gently and place in the slow cooker. Add the water and close the lid. Cook for 2 hours on High. Serve the side dish hot!

Nutrition: calories 52, fat 3, fiber 2, carbs 6.4, protein 1

Layered Mushrooms

Prep time: 25 minutes | Cooking time: 6 hours | Servings: 6

Ingredients:
- 7 oz white mushrooms, sliced
- 1 eggplant, peeled, sliced
- 1 tablespoon dried dill
- 1 teaspoon cayenne pepper
- 1 onion, grated
- 5 tablespoons almond milk, unsweetened
- 1 oz butter

Directions:
Mix the dried dill, cayenne pepper, and butter. Stir the mixture until smooth. Melt the butter mixture. Make a layer of the slice eggplant in the slow cooker. Brush it with some of the butter mixture. Make the layer of the mushrooms and top it with the grated onion. Add all the remaining butter mixture and almond milk. Close the lid and cook the meal for 6 hours on Low. Let the cooked mushrooms rest for 15-20 minutes. Serve!

Nutrition: calories 98, fat 7.1, fiber 3.8, carbs 8.4, protein 2.5

Rutabaga Wedges

Prep time: 15 minutes | Cooking time: 2 hours | Servings: 3

Ingredients:
- 8 oz rutabaga
- 1 tablespoon olive oil
- 1 teaspoon butter
- 1 teaspoon dried dill
- 1 teaspoon minced garlic
- 4 tablespoons almond milk, unsweetened
- ½ teaspoon salt

Directions:
Mix the olive oil, butter, dried dill, minced garlic, almond milk, and salt. Whisk the mixture until homogenous. Then slice the rutabaga into wedges. Sprinkle the rutabaga wedges with the olive oil mixture from each side and place them in the slow cooker. Close the lid and cook the side dish for 2 hours on High.

Nutrition: calories 127, fat 10.9, fiber 2.4, carbs 7.8, protein 1.5

Thai Cabbage

Prep time: 15 minutes | Cooking time: 6 hours | Servings: 4

Ingredients:
- 1 tablespoon coconut oil
- 7 oz white cabbage, shredded
- 1 tablespoon curry paste
- 3 tablespoons water
- 1 teaspoon salt
- 3 tablespoons butter, melted

Directions:
Mix the curry paste and water. Add salt and coconut oil and whisk. Place the shredded cabbage in the slow cooker. Sprinkle it with the curry paste mixture. Add the butter and stir the vegetables gently. Close the lid and cook the cabbage on Low for 6 hours. When the time is done, let the cabbage rest for 10 minutes. Serve it!

Nutrition: calories 143, fat 14.3, fiber 1.2, carbs 4, protein 0.9

Eggplant Hash

Prep time: 20 minutes | Cooking time: 3 hours | Servings: 6

Ingredients:
- 2 eggplants, peeled, chopped
- 1 onion, diced
- 5 oz white mushrooms, chopped
- ½ cup water
- 1 oz butter
- 1 teaspoon cayenne pepper

Directions:
Place the eggplants and onion in the slow cooker. Sprinkle the vegetables with the chopped mushrooms, water, butter, and cayenne pepper. Stir the vegetable gently and close the lid. Cook theeggplants hash for 3 hours on High. When the eggplants hash is cooked, let it chill for 10 minutes. Serve it!

Nutrition: calories 93, fat 4.3, fiber 7.2, carbs 13.4, protein 2.8

Creamy Eggplant Salad

Prep time: 15 minutes | Cooking time: 3 hours | Servings: 5

Ingredients:
- 1 eggplant, peeled
- 1 teaspoon salt
- 2 bell peppers, chopped
- 1 jalapeno pepper, chopped
- 1 tablespoon almond milk, unsweetened
- ¾ cup coconut milk, unsweetened
- 1 tablespoon almond flour
- 1 tablespoon dried dill

Directions:
Chop the eggplant and place it in the slow cooker. Add chopped jalapeno pepper, almond milk, coconut milk, almond flour, and dried dill. Stir the vegetables gently and close the lid. Cook the vegetables for 3 hourson High. Transfercooked vegetable mixture into the salad bowl. Add chopped bell peppers and stir well. Serve the salad!

Nutrition: calories 123, fat 8.9, fiber 4.8, carbs 11.5, protein 2.4

Slow Cooker Broccoli Rabe

Prep time: 15 minutes | Cooking time: 1 hour | Servings: 3

Ingredients:
- 4 oz bacon, chopped, cooked
- 10 oz broccoli rabe, chopped
- 2 oz Parmesan, grated
- 1 teaspoon salt
- 1 teaspoon chili flakes
- 1 teaspoon ground black pepper
- ¼ cup almond milk, unsweetened
- 1 teaspoon butter

Directions:
Mix the chopped broccoli rabe and cooked bacon. Transfer the mixture to the slow cooker. Add the grated Parmesan, salt, chili flakes, ground black pepper and almond milk. Stir gently and add butter. Close the lid and cook the meal for 1 hour on High. Transfer the hot cooked meal onto serving plates and

Nutrition: calories 347, fat 25.9, fiber 0.6, carbs 6.2, protein 22.9

Soft Keto Kale Salad

Prep time: 15 minutes | Cooking time: 30 minutes | Servings: 4

Ingredients:
- 6 oz bacon, chopped, cooked
- 1 oz almond, chopped
- 1 tablespoon olive oil
- 1 cup Italian dark-leaf kale, chopped
- ¾ cup almond milk, unsweetened
- 1 cucumber, chopped
- 1 garlic clove, diced

Directions:
Place the chopped kale, almond milk, and diced garlic in the slow cooker. Close the lid and cook the kale for 30 minutes on High. Meanwhile, place the chopped cucumbers in the salad bowl. Add olive oil, bacon, and chopped almond. When the kale is cooked, transfer it immediately to the salad bowl and stir. Serve it warm!

Nutrition: calories 423, fat 35.6, fiber 2.8, carbs 8.4, protein 19.3

Keto Leeks

Prep time: 10 minutes | Cooking time: 2 hours | Servings: 3

Ingredients:
- 8 oz leek, sliced
- 1 tablespoon butter
- 1 tablespoon full-fat cream cheese
- 1 teaspoon ground black pepper
- ¼ teaspoon minced garlic

Directions:
Place the sliced leek, butter, creamcheese, ground black pepper, and minced garlic in the slow cooker. Stir the ingredients and close the lid. Cook theleeks for 2 hours on High. Stir the cooked leeks and serve!

Nutrition: calories 52, fat 2.5, fiber 0.9, carbs 6.9, protein 1.2

Green Bean and Avocado Salad

Prep time: 15 minutes | Cooking time: 2 hours | Servings: 4

Ingredients:
- 1 avocado, peeled, pitted
- 8 oz green beans
- 1 cup water
- 1 teaspoon ground black pepper
- 1 teaspoon salt
- 1 cucumber, chopped
- 1 teaspoon butter
- 1 oz walnuts, chopped
- 1 tablespoon olive oil

Directions:

Put the green beans in the slow cooker. Add the water, ground black pepper, and salt. Close the lid and cook the green beans for 2 hours on High. Meanwhile, chop the avocado and put it in a salad bowl. Add the chopped cucumber, walnuts, and olive oil to the salad bowl as well Add the cooked warm green beans and stir the salad. it!

Nutrition: calories 216, fat 18.6, fiber 6.3, carbs 12.1, protein 4.3

Red Cabbage Slices

Prep time: 15 minutes | Cooking time: 1 hour | Servings: 4

Ingredients:
- 14 oz red cabbage
- 4 tablespoons olive oil
- 1 teaspoon dried oregano
- 1 teaspoon dried dill
- 4 tablespoons water
- 1 teaspoon salt

Directions:

Slice the red cabbage and sprinkle it with the olive oil, dried oregano, dried dill, and salt. Stir well. Transfer the red cabbage mix into the slow cooker. Add the water and close the lid. Cook the red cabbage for 1 hour on High. Serve the cabbage immediately!

Nutrition: calories 147, fat 14.2, fiber 2.7, carbs 6.1, protein 1.4

Cauliflower Puree with Parmesan

Prep time: 15 minutes | Cooking time: 6 hours | Servings: 5

Ingredients:
- 1-pound cauliflower
- 1 cup water
- 2 tablespoons butter
- 2 oz Parmesan, grated

Directions:

Chop the cauliflower and place it in the slow cooker. Add the water and close the lid. Cook the cauliflower for 6 hours on Low. Strain the cauliflower and place it in the blender. Add the butter and blend it until you get a smooth puree. Transfer the cauliflower puree to serving plates and sprinkle with grated Parmesan. Serve it!

Nutrition: calories 100, fat 7.1, fiber 2.3, carbs 5.2, protein 5.5

Cauliflower Croquettes

Prep time: 20 minutes | Cooking time: 2 hours | Servings: 4

Ingredients:
- 1 egg
- 8 oz cauliflower, grated
- 1 teaspoon salt
- 3 tablespoons almond flour
- 1 tablespoon butter
- ½ teaspoon cayenne pepper

Directions:
Beat the egg in a bowl. Add grated cauliflower, salt, and cayenne pepper to the whisked egg and stir. Then make small balls from the mixture and coat them with the almond flour. Toss the butter in the slow cooker. Add the cauliflower croquettes to the slow cooker as well and cook them for 2 hours on High. Let the cooked croquettes cool for at least 10 minutes. Serve!

Nutrition: calories 176, fat 14.6, fiber 3.7, carbs 7.7, protein 7.1

Grated Zucchini with Cheese

Prep time: 15 minutes | Cooking time: 30 minutes | Servings: 4

Ingredients:
- 2 oz Parmesan cheese, grated
- 1 zucchini, grated
- 1 teaspoon ground black pepper
- 1 tablespoon olive oil
- 1 teaspoon dried dill
- 4 tablespoons water

Directions:
Mix the grated zucchini, ground black pepper, and dried dill. Stir the mixture and transfer it to the slow cooker. Add water and olive oil. Then sprinkle a layer of Parmesan cheese over the zucchini and close the lid. Cook the meal for 30 minutes on High. Serve the dish hot!

Nutrition: calories 85, fat 6.7, fiber 0.7, carbs 2.6, protein 5.3

Cheesy Spaghetti Squash

Prep time: 25 minutes | Cooking time: 4 hours | Servings: 2

Ingredients:
- 10 oz spaghetti squash, peeled and seeded
- 1 tablespoon butter
- ½ teaspoon thyme
- 1 teaspoon paprika
- 1/3 cup water
- 2 oz Parmesan, sliced

Directions:
Grate the spaghetti squash and place it in the slow cooker. Add the butter, thyme, paprika, and water. Stir the mixture gently with a spoon. Then cover the squash with the sliced cheese and close the lid. Cook the meal for 4 hours on Low. Let the cooked squash rest for 15 minutes. Serve it!

Nutrition: calories 190, fat 12.8, fiber 0.5, carbs 11.6, protein 10.3

Pesto Spaghetti Squash

Prep time: 15 minutes | Cooking time: 6 hours | Servings: 4

Ingredients:
- 1 cup spinach
- 2 tablespoons olive oil
- 1 oz pumpkin seeds, crushed
- 1-pound spaghetti squash
- 1 teaspoon butter
- ¾ cup water

Directions:
Chop the spaghetti squash and put it in the slow cooker. Add butter and water. Close the lid and cook for 6 hours on Low. Meanwhile, chop the spinach and place it in the blender. Add olive oil and pumpkin seeds. Blend the mixture until smooth. When the spaghetti squash is cooked, transfer it into the serving bowls and sprinkle with the spinach (pesto) mixture. Serve it!

Nutrition: calories 144, fat 11.9, fiber 0.5, carbs 9.4, protein 2.7

Zucchini Slices with Mozzarella

Prep time: 15 minutes | Cooking time: 1 hour | Servings: 4

Ingredients:
- 3 oz Mozzarella, sliced
- 1 zucchini, sliced
- 1 tablespoon olive oil
- 1 teaspoon butter
- 1 tablespoon coconut flakes, unsweetened
- 1 teaspoon minced garlic

Directions:
Sprinkle the zucchini slices with the olive oil, coconut flakes, and minced garlic. Place the zucchini slices in a flat layer on the bottom of the slow cooker along with the butter. Place a piece of mozzarella on top of each zucchini slice. Close the lid and cook the meal for 1 hour on High. Serve hot!

Nutrition: calories 112, fat 8.7, fiber 0.7, carbs 2.8, protein 6.7

Kale Mash with Blue Cheese

Prep time: 15 minutes | Cooking time: 5 hours | Servings: 3

Ingredients:
- 3 oz Blue cheese
- 1 cup Italian dark-leaf kale
- ¾ cup almond milk, unsweetened
- 1 tablespoon butter
- 1 teaspoon salt
- 1 teaspoon ground black pepper

Directions:
Chop the kale and place it in the slow cooker. Add almond milk, salt, and ground black pepper. Close the lid and cook the kale for 5 hours on Low. Meanwhile, chop Blue cheese and butter. Combine the cooked kale with the butter and stir it until butter is melted. Add the Blue cheese and stir it gently. Serve!

Nutrition: calories 285, fat 26.3, fiber 1.8, carbs 6.8, protein 8.2

Black Soybeans

Prep time: 10 minutes | Cooking time: 7 hours | Servings: 6

Ingredients:
- 10 oz black soybeans
- 2 cups water
- 1 teaspoon salt
- 1 teaspoon chili flakes
- 1 tablespoon dried dill
- 1 teaspoon butter

Directions:

Place the black soybeans, water, salt, and chili flakes in the slow cooker. Close the lid and cook the soybeans for 7 hours on Low. Place the cooked soybeans in the bowls and combine with butter. Stir and serve!

Nutrition: calories 218, fat 10.1, fiber 4.5, carbs 14.6, protein 17.4

Marinated Fennel Bulb

Prep time: 10 minutes | Cooking time: 4 hours | Servings: 2

Ingredients:
- 8 oz fennel bulb
- 1 tablespoon apple cider vinegar
- 1 garlic clove, diced
- 1 teaspoon dried oregano
- 5 tablespoons almond milk, unsweetened
- 1 teaspoon butter

Directions:

Chop the fennel bulb roughly and sprinkle it with the apple cider vinegar, diced garlic clove, and dried oregano. Stir and let marinate for 15 minutes. Place the chopped fennel in the slow cooker. Add butter and almond milk. Close the lid and cook for 4 hours on Low. Then chill the cooked fennel slightly and serve!

Nutrition: calories 144, fat 11.2, fiber 4.7, carbs 11.4, protein 2.5

Pumpkin Cubes

Prep time: 25 minutes | Cooking time: 5 hours | Servings: 2

Ingredients:
- 8 oz pumpkin
- 1 teaspoon ground cinnamon
- 1 teaspoon liquid stevia
- 1 teaspoon butter
- 2 tablespoons water
- 1 teaspoon ground ginger

Directions:

Peel the pumpkin and chop it. Place the choppedpumpkin in the slow cooker. Add ground cinnamon, liquid stevia, and ground ginger. Stir it gently and add water and butter. Close the lid and cook the pumpkin for 5 hours on Low. When the pumpkin is cooked, it will be nice and tender. Let it rest for 10 minutes.

Nutrition: calories 61, fat 2.3, fiber 4, carbs 10.7, protein 1.4

Snacks and Appetizers

Wrapped Avocado Sticks

Prep time: 15 minutes | Cooking time: 2 hours | Servings: 7

Ingredients:
- 5 oz bacon, sliced
- 1 avocado, pitted
- 1 teaspoon paprika
- ½ teaspoon salt
- 2 tablespoons butter

Directions:
Cut the avocado into the medium sticks. Sprinkle the avocado sticks with the paprika and salt. Wrap the avocado sticks in the sliced bacon. Place the avocado sticks in the slow cooker and add the butter. Close the lid and cook the snack for 2 hours on High. Cool the cooked avocado sticks to room temperature and serve!

Nutrition: calories 198, fat 17.4, fiber 2, carbs 2.9, protein 8.

Deviled Eggs

Prep time: 10 minutes | Cooking time: 2.5 hours | Servings: 4

Ingredients:
- 2 eggs
- 1 cup water
- 1 teaspoon paprika
- ¼ teaspoon chili pepper
- 1 tablespoon butter
- ½ teaspoon minced garlic

Directions:
Place eggs, water in the slow cooker, and close the lid. Cook the eggs for 2.5 hours on High. Peel the eggs and cut into halves. Remove the egg yolks and place them in the blender. Add the paprika, butter, chili pepper, and minced garlic. Blend the egg yolks until smooth. Fill the egg whites with the egg yolk mixture. Serve!

Nutrition: calories 59, fat 5.1, fiber 0.2, carbs 0.6, protein 2.9

Turkey Meatballs

Prep time: 15 minutes | Cooking time: 3 hours | Servings: 6

Ingredients:
- 10 oz ground turkey
- 1 teaspoon dried basil
- 1 teaspoon minced garlic
- 1 teaspoon ground black pepper
- ¾ cup almond milk, unsweetened
- 1 teaspoon oregano
- 1 tablespoon almond flour

Directions:
Mix the ground turkey, dried basil, minced garlic, ground black pepper, oregano, and almond flour. Stir the mixture until well blended. Pour the almond milk into the slow cooker. Make medium meatballs from the turkey mix and put them in the slow cooker. Cook the meatballs for 3 hours on High. Let the cooked meatballs cool slightly. Serve!

Nutrition: calories 190, fat 14.7, fiber 1.4, carbs 3.2, protein 14.7

Chicken and Cauliflower Pizza

Prep time: 15minutes | Cooking time: 5hours | Servings: 6

Ingredients:
- 3 oz cauliflower, chopped
- 4 tablespoons almond flour
- 1 egg, beaten
- ¼ teaspoon salt
- ¼ tea spoon ground black pepper
- 2 oz ground chicken
- 1 teaspoon butter

Directions:

Mix the almond flour and beaten egg. Add salt and ground black pepper. Knead into a smooth dough. Roll out the dough in the shape of pizza crust. Rub the slow cooker bowl with the butter and place the pizza crust inside the bowl. Place the ground chicken on top of the pizza crust. Sprinkle the ground chicken with the chopped cauliflower and close the lid. Cook the pizza for 5 hours on Low. Let the cooked pizza cool slightly then slice it into servings and

Nutrition: calories 144, fat 11.4, fiber 2.4, carbs 4.9, protein 4.8

Cauliflower Bites

Prep time: 15 minutes | Cooking time: 2 hours | Servings: 4Ingredients:

Ingredients:
- 7 oz cauliflower florets
- 1 egg, beaten
- 1 tablespoon almond flour
- ¼ teaspoon chili pepper
- 2 tablespoons butter

Directions:

Mix the almond flour and chili pepper together. Dip the cauliflower florets into the whisked egg. Then, coat them in the almond flour mixture. Toss the butter into the slow cooker. Add the dipped cauliflower florets and close the lid Cook the cauliflower for 2 hours on High. When the cauliflower bites are cooked, let them cool slightly. Serve!

Nutrition: calories 119, fat 10.4, fiber 2, carbs 4.2, protein 3.9

Wrapped Prawns in Bacon

Prep time: 15 minutes | Cooking time: 2 hours | Servings: 2

Ingredients:
- 6 oz prawns, peeled
- 2 oz bacon, sliced
- 1 teaspoon butter
- ¼ teaspoon minced garlic

Directions:

Mix the minced garlic and butter. Rub the prawns in the butter mixture. Wrap them in the sliced bacon. Transfer the prawns to the slow cooker and cook for 2 hours on High. Serve the cooked prawns and

Nutrition: calories 272, fat 15.2, fiber 0, carbs 1.8, protein 29.9

Buffalo Chicken Wings

Prep time: 15 minutes | Cooking time: 7 hours | Servings: 4

Ingredients:
- 10 oz chicken wings
- ¾ cup hot sauce
- 1 teaspoon minced garlic
- 2 tablespoons butter
- 1 teaspoon cayenne pepper
- 1 teaspoon paprika

Directions:
Mix the hot sauce, minced garlic, butter, cayenne pepper, and paprika. Mix the chicken wings with the sauce. Place the chicken wings and all the sauce in the slow cooker. Cook the chicken wings for 7 hours on Low. Serve the chicken wings immediately!

Nutrition: calories 194, fat 11.3, fiber 0.5, carbs 1.5, protein 21

Eggplant Fries

Prep time: 20 minutes | Cooking time: 1.5 hours | Servings: 4

Ingredients:
- 1 eggplant
- 1 teaspoon paprika
- ½ teaspoon turmeric
- ½ teaspoon salt
- 1 tablespoon butter, melted
- ¼ cup coconut flour

Directions:
Cut the eggplant into medium sticks. Sprinkle the eggplant sticks with the paprika, turmeric, and salt. Dip the eggplant sticks in the melted butter and coat in the coconut flour. Place the eggplant sticks in the slow cooker and cook for 1.5 hours on High. Let the cooked eggplant fries cool slightly.

Nutrition: calories 87, fat 4.2, fiber 6.8, carbs 11.2, protein 2.3

Parmesan Green Beans

Prep time: 10 minutes | Cooking time: 3 hours | Servings: 2

Ingredients:
- 2 oz Parmesan, grated
- 5 oz green beans
- ¼ cup almond milk, unsweetened
- 1 teaspoon paprika

Directions:
Place the green beans in the slow cooker. Add almond milk and paprika. Stir and cook the green beans for 2 hours on High. Sprinkle the green beans with Parmesan cheese and cook for 1 hour more on High. Chill the cooked green beans slightly and serve!

Nutrition: calories 185, fat 13.5, fiber 3.5, carbs 8.3, protein 11.2

Zucchini Fries

Prep time: 15 minutes | Cooking time: 2 hours | Servings: 4

Ingredients:
- 1 zucchini
- ¼ cup almond flour
- 1 egg
- 1 tablespoon butter
- ½ cup almond flour
- 1 teaspoon onion powder

Directions:
Wash the zucchini well and cut into sticks. Beat the egg in a bowl. Dip the zucchini sticks in the whisked egg then sprinkle the zucchini sticks with the onion powder and dip them in the almond flour. Transfer the zucchini sticks into the slow cooker. Add butter and cook the zucchini for 2 hours on High. Serve the cooked zucchini fries immediately!

Nutrition: calories 61, fat 5, fiber 0.8, carbs 2.6, protein2.4

Cauliflower Fritters

Prep time: 15 minutes | Cooking time: 2.5 hours | Servings: 6

Ingredients:
- 8 oz cauliflower
- 1 egg
- 2 tablespoons almond flour
- 1 tablespoon butter
- 1 teaspoon dried oregano

Directions:
Chop the cauliflower roughly and place them in a blender. Blend the cauliflower until smooth and transfer into a mixing bowl. Add the almond flour and dried oregano. Add the beaten egg and stir it well. Make into medium fritters. Place the butter in the slow cooker and add the fritters. Cook the cauliflower fritters for 2.5 hours on High. Serve the meal!

Nutrition: calories 91, fat 7.4, fiber 2.1, carbs 4.2, protein 3.7

Zucchini Latkes

Prep time: 15 minutes | Cooking time: 2 hours | Servings: 3

Ingredients:
- 1 zucchini, grated
- 1 onion, grated
- 1 teaspoon butter
- 1 tablespoon almond flour
- 1 teaspoon salt

Directions:
Mix grated zucchini, onion, and salt. Add almond flour and stir the mixture until smooth. Add the butter to the slow cooker. Make the medium latkes using 2 spoons. Place them in the slow cooker and close the lid. Cook the zucchini latkes for 2 hours on High. Transfer the latkes to a platter and serve!

Nutrition: calories 90, fat 6.1, fiber 2.5, carbs 7.6, protein 3.2

Zucchini Tots with Cheese

Prep time: 15 minutes | Cooking time: 3 hours | Servings: 6

Ingredients:
- 1 zucchini, grated
- 3 oz Parmesan, grated
- 1 teaspoon dried dill
- 1 teaspoon dried oregano
- ½ teaspoon salt
- 1 egg
- 1 tablespoon almond flour
- 1 tablespoon butter

Directions:
Mix the zucchini, Parmesan, dried dill, dried oregano, salt, almond flour, and beaten egg. Stir the mixture until smooth. Form small tots and place them in the slow cooker. The mixture should not be liquid so add more almond flour if needed in order to form the tots. Add butter to the slow cooker and close the lid. Cook the zucchini tots for 3 hours on High. Chill the zucchini tots to room temperature and serve!

Nutrition: calories 106, fat 8.1, fiber 1, carbs 2.9, protein 7

Spicy & Salty Keto Nuts

Prep time: 15 minutes | Cooking time: 1 hour | Servings: 2

Ingredients:
- 1 oz walnuts, crushed
- 1 oz hazelnuts, crushed
- 1 oz pumpkin seeds
- 1 teaspoon cayenne pepper
- 1 teaspoon salt
- 1 teaspoon olive oil
- 1 teaspoon garlic powder
- 1 Tablespoon Butter

Directions:
Place the walnuts, hazelnuts, and pumpkin seeds in the slow cooker. Sprinkle them with the cayenne pepper, salt, olive oil, butter and garlic powder. Stir the mixture gently and close the lid. Cook the nuts for 1 hour on High. Then let the cooked mixture chill for 10 minutes. Serve!

Nutrition: calories 292, fat 30, fiber 3.3, carbs 7.8, protein 9.4

Jalapeno Fritters

Prep time: 15 minutes | Cooking time: 3 hours | Servings: 4

Ingredients:
- 4 jalapeno peppers
- 1 egg, beaten
- 1 teaspoon cayenne pepper
- ½ teaspoon salt
- 2 tablespoons almond flour
- 1 teaspoon paprika
- ½ teaspoon garlic powder
- 1 teaspoon butter

Directions:
Mix the beaten egg, cayenne pepper, salt, and almond flour. Add paprika and garlic powder and whisk the mixture until smooth. Melt the butter and place it in the slow cooker. Coat the jalapeno peppers in the egg batter well and transfer into the slow cooker. Cook the peppers for 3 hours on High. Let the cooked jalapenos cool slightly.

Nutrition: calories 114, fat 9.4, fiber 2.4, carbs 4.9, protein 4.8

Onion Rings

Prep time: 15 minutes | Cooking time: 2 hours | Servings: 6

Ingredients:
- 1 big onion, peeled
- 1/3 cup almond flour
- 1 egg, beaten
- 2 tablespoons almond milk, unsweetened
- 1 tablespoon coconut flakes
- 1 teaspoon ground black pepper
- 1 teaspoon butter

Directions:
Slice the onion and separate it into the rings. Mix the almond milk and ground black pepper. Add the beaten egg and whisk. Dip the onion rings in the whisked egg mixture then coat the onion rings in the almond flour. Toss the butter into the slow cooker and add the onion rings. Cook the onion rings for 2 hours on High. Serve the onion rings hot!

Nutrition: calories 50, fat 3.7, fiber 1, carbs 3.4, protein 1.7

Keto Tortillas with Cheese

Prep time: 15 minutes | Cooking time: 1 hour | Servings: 4

Ingredients:
- 4 egg whites
- 4 tablespoons almond flour
- 3 tablespoons water
- 1 teaspoon olive oil
- ¾ teaspoon baking soda
- ¼ teaspoon garlic powder
- ¼ teaspoon chili flakes
- 2 oz Parmesan, grated

Directions:
Whisk the egg whites gently then add almond flour and water. Add baking soda, garlic powder, and chili flakes. Knead the mix into a smooth dough. Roll out the dough into medium sized tortilla. Then pour the olive oil in the slow cooker and add the tortillas. Sprinkle the tortilla with the grated cheese and close the lid. Cook the tortilla for 1 hour on High. Serve the cooked snack hot!

Nutrition: calories 233, fat 18.3, fiber 3, carbs 6.9, protein 14.2

Sweet and Spicy Chicken Wings

Prep time: 15 minutes | Cooking time: 6 hours | Servings: 4

Ingredients:
- 4 chicken wings
- 1 tablespoon coconut flakes, unsweetened
- ½ teaspoon chili flakes
- 1 tablespoon butter
- ½ teaspoon thyme
- ½ teaspoon minced garlic
- 1 teaspoon dried dill

Directions:
Mix the chili flakes, thyme, minced garlic, and dried dill together. Sprinkle the chicken wings with the spices and coconut flakes. Place the butter and chicken wings in the slow cooker and close the lid. Cook the chicken wings for 6 hours on Low. Let the chicken wings cool a little. Serve warm!

Nutrition: calories 33, fat 3.4, fiber 0.2, carbs 0.5, protein 0.4

Ground Chicken Pepper Meatballs
Prep time: 15 minutes | Cooking time: 3 hours | Servings: 4

Ingredients:
- 11 oz ground chicken
- 1 bell pepper
- 1 teaspoon salt
- 1 teaspoon butter
- 1 teaspoon dried dill
- 1 teaspoon dried oregano
- 1 egg yolk
- ½ teaspoon ground ginger

Directions:
Chop the bell pepper and place it in a blender. Blend the bell pepper until smooth. Mix the bell pepper puree with the ground chicken. Add salt, dried dill, dried oregano, and ground ginger. Add egg yolk and stir carefully. Make small meatballs and place them in the slow cooker. Add butter and close the lid. Cook the meatballs for 3 hours. Serve the appetizer hot!

Nutrition: calories 182, fat 8, fiber 0.6, carbs 2.9, protein 23.6

Pork Nuggets
Prep time: 20 minutes | Cooking time: 4 hours | Servings: 4

Ingredients:
- 8 oz pork loin
- 1 egg white
- 1 teaspoon turmeric
- 1 teaspoon paprika
- ¼ teaspoon salt
- 1 teaspoon butter
- ¾ cup almond flour

Directions:
Cut the pork loin into one inch pieces. Whisk the egg and combine it with the paprika, turmeric, and salt. Dip the pork cubes into the egg mixture then coat the pork in the almond flour. Place the nuggets in the slow cooker and add butter. Close the lid and cook the nuggets for 4 hours on High. Cool the nuggets slightly. Serve!

Nutrition: calories 183, fat 11.6, fiber 0.9, carbs 1.9, protein 17.7

Meat Balls with Mozzarella
Prep time: 20 minutes | Cooking time: 3 hours | Servings: 5

Ingredients:
- 3 oz Mozzarella
- 7 oz ground pork
- ¼ teaspoon chili flakes
- ½ teaspoon salt
- 1 teaspoon dried dill
- ¾ cup water
- 1 tablespoon coconut flakes, unsweetened

Directions:
Chop the Mozzarella into small cubes. Mix the ground pork, chili flakes, salt, dried dill, and coconut flakes. Stir the ground pork mixture well. Make into medium balls and place a piece of Mozzarella inside every ball. Put the meatballs in the slow cooker and add ¾ cup of water. Cook for 3 hours on High. the meatballs hot!

Nutrition: calories 109, fat 4.7, fiber 0.1, carbs 1.6, protein 15.3

Pulled Pork

Prep time: 20 minutes | Cooking time: 7 hours | Servings: 8

Ingredients:
- 1-pound pork shoulder
- 1 cup water
- ¼ teaspoon peppercorn
- ¼ teaspoon ground ginger
- 1 teaspoon paprika
- ¼ teaspoon cayenne pepper
- 1 teaspoon tomato paste
- 1 tablespoon butter

Directions:
Rub the pork shoulder with the cayenne pepper, peppercorns, ground ginger, paprika, cayenne pepper, and tomato paste. Let the pork shoulder marinate for 20 minutes in the fridge. Transfer the pork shoulder into the slow cooker. Add the butter and water. Close the lid and cook the pork shoulder for 7 hours on Low. Remove the pork shoulder from the slow cooker and shred it with two forks. Place the pork in a bowl and add ½ of the remaining liquid from the slow cooker. Stir the pulled pork and serve with keto bread, if desired.

Nutrition: calories 181, fat 13.6, fiber 0.2, carbs 0.5, protein 13.3

Crunchy Bacon

Prep time: 8 minutes | Cooking time: 1.5 hours | Servings: 6

Ingredients:
- 7 oz bacon, sliced
- 1 teaspoon liquid stevia
- ½ teaspoon butter

Directions:
Place the butter in the slow cooker. Add the sliced bacon and sprinkle it with the liquid stevia. Close the lid and cook the bacon for 1 hour on High. Turn the bacon over onto the other side and cook it for 30 minutes more on High. Serve the bacon chilled.

Nutrition: calories 182, fat 14.1, fiber 0, carbs 0.5, protein 12.3

Seasoned Mini Meatballs

Prep time: 20 minutes | Cooking time: 3 hours | Servings: 8

Ingredients:
- ¼ cup spinach
- 1 egg
- 1 tablespoon almond flour
- ½ teaspoon salt
- 1 tablespoon olive oil
- 1 teaspoon paprika
- 8 oz ground beef
- 1 teaspoon dried oregano

Directions:
Beat the egg in a mixing bowl. Blend the spinach in a blender until smooth. Add the blended spinach into the whisked egg. Add almond flour, salt, paprika, ground beef, and dried oregano and mix well. Make mini meatballs using 2 teaspoons to form the balls and place them in the slow cooker. Add olive oil and cook for 3 hours on High. Chill the meatballs slightly and serve!

Nutrition: calories 97, fat 5.9, fiber 0.6, carbs 1.1, protein 10.1

Mini Chicken Meatballs

Prep time: 20 minutes | Cooking time: 2.5hours | Servings: 4

Ingredients:
- 1 teaspoon hot sauce
- 7 oz ground chicken
- ½ onion, grated
- 1 teaspoon turmeric
- 1 teaspoon liquid stevia
- 1 teaspoon butter
- 1 egg white

Directions:
Mix the ground chicken and grated onion. Add hot sauce, turmeric, liquid stevia, and egg white. Stir the mixture with a spoon. Form the meatballs and place them in the slow cooker. Add the butter and close the lid. Cook the chicken meatballs for 2.5 hours on High. Transfer the chicken meatballs onto a platter and serve!

Nutrition: calories 115, fat 4.7, fiber 0.4, carbs 1.7, protein 15.5

Spinach Rolls

Prep time: 15 minutes | Cooking time: 3 hours | Servings: 4

Ingredients:
- 1 cup spinach leaves
- 6 oz ground chicken
- ¼ teaspoon salt
- ¼ teaspoon paprika
- ¼ teaspoon turmeric
- 1 teaspoon butter

Directions:
Mix the ground chicken, salt, paprika, and turmeric. Place the ground chicken mixture in the slow cooker. Add the butter and cook on High for 3 hours. Stir the cooked ground chicken mixture. Place the ground chicken mixture in the spinach leaves and roll them up, enclosing the meat inside the leaf. Secure the rolls with the toothpicks and serve!

Nutrition: calories 92, fat 4.2, fiber 0.3, carbs 0.4, protein 12.6

Pork Belly Bites

Prep time: 10 minutes | Cooking time: 3 hours | Servings: 4

Ingredients:
- 7 oz pork belly
- ¼ teaspoon thyme
- ¼ teaspoon paprika
- ¼ teaspoonground coriander
- 1 tablespoon butter

Directions:
Cut the pork belly into bite sized pieces and rub them with the thyme, paprika, and ground coriander. Place the butter in the slow cooker. Add the pork belly bites to the slow cooker and cook for 3 hours on High.   while hot!

Nutrition: calories 255, fat 16.3, fiber 0.1, carbs 0.1, protein 23

Sweet Brussel Sprouts

Prep time: 15 minutes | Cooking time: 4 hours | Servings: 6

Ingredients:
- 8 oz Brussel sprouts
- 1 teaspoon Erythritol
- 1 teaspoon mustard seeds
- 1 teaspoon olive oil
- 5 oz Parmesan, chopped

Directions:
Mix the mustard seeds and Erythritol. Add olive oil and stir it. Place Brussel sprouts in the slow cooker and add olive oil mixture. Stir and then cook the vegetable for 4 hours on Low. Use toothpicks to skewer a piece of the chopped cheese and a Brussel sprout for easy serving. Serve!

Nutrition: calories 101, fat 6.1, fiber 1.5, carbs 5.3, protein 9

Mushroom Skewers

Prep time: 15 minutes | Cooking time: 4 hours | Servings: 4

Ingredients:
- 6 oz white mushrooms, roughly chopped
- 1 eggplant, peeled
- 1 tablespoon butter, melted
- 1 teaspoon minced garlic
- 1 teaspoon dried parsley
- ½ teaspoon ground black pepper

Directions:
Chop the eggplant roughly. Mix the white mushrooms, eggplant, minced garlic, dried parsley, and ground black pepper. Stir the vegetables and slide them onto skewers. Place the skewers in the slow cooker and add butter. Cook the skewers for 4 hours on Low. Serve the meal!

Nutrition: calories 65, fat 3.2, fiber 4.6, carbs 8.6, protein 2.6

Tilapia Bites

Prep time: 15 minutes | Cooking time: 2 hours | Servings: 4

Ingredients:
- 8 oz tilapia fillet
- ½ teaspoon ground black pepper
- ½ teaspoon paprika
- 1 tablespoon almond milk, unsweetened
- ½ teaspoon thyme
- 1 tablespoon olive oil

Directions:
Cut the tilapia fillet into bites. Sprinkle the fish with the ground black pepper, thyme, and paprika. Then add the fish into the slow cooker. Add olive oil and almond milk and close the lid. Cook the tilapia bites for 2 hours on High. Then let the cooked tilapia bites cool until room temperature and serve!

Nutrition: calories 87, fat 5, fiber 0.3, carbs 0.6, protein 10.7

Stuffed Mushrooms

Prep time: 15 minutes | Cooking time: 2 hours | Servings: 4

Ingredients:
- 6 oz mushrooms, stems removed
- 1 tablespoon butter
- ¼ cup spinach, chopped
- 1 teaspoon cayenne pepper

Directions:
Blend the chopped spinach and combine it with the cayenne pepper and butter. Fill the mushrooms, stuffing the hole where the stem use to be, with the butter mixture and place in the slow cooker. Cook the mushrooms for 2 hours on High. Serve the cooked mushrooms immediately.

Nutrition: calories 36, fat 3.1, fiber 0.6, carbs 1.7, protein 1.5

Asian Pork with Keto Tortillas

Prep time: 40 minutes | Cooking time: 6 hours | Servings: 6

Ingredients:
- 6 keto tortillas
- 9 oz pork tenderloin
- 1 tablespoon apple cider vinegar
- 1 teaspoon olive oil
- ½ teaspoon thyme
- 1 teaspoon curry paste
- 1 teaspoon sesame seeds
- ¼ cup water

Directions:
Chop the pork tenderloins and sprinkle them with the apple cider vinegar, olive oil, thyme, curry paste, and sesame seeds. Stir the meat well and let sit for 30 minutes to marinate. Transfer the meat to the slow cooker and add water. Close the lid and cook the meat for 6 hours on Low. Place the cooked meat on the tortillas and roll. Serve warm!

Nutrition: calories 227, fat 11, fiber 4.1, carbs 8.4, protein 23.3

Caprese Meatballs

Prep time: 15 minutes | Cooking time: 2 hours | Servings: 6

Ingredients:
- 7 oz ground turkey
- 1 egg
- 3 tablespoons almond flour
- ¼ teaspoon garlic powder
- 1 oz dried tomatoes, chopped
- 1 tablespoons dried basil
- 1 teaspoon butter

Directions:
Beat the egg into the ground turkey. Add the almond flour and garlic powder. Add the dried basil and stir the turkey mixture. Roll into meatballs. Place the meatballs in the slow cooker and add butter. Close the lid and cook the meatballs for 2 hours on High. Then slide the meatballs onto the skewers. Add the dried tomatoes to the skewers and serve!

Nutrition: calories 162, fat 12, fiber 1.6, carbs 3.3, protein 13.1

Chicken Tenders

Prep time: 15 minutes | Cooking time: 2.5 hours | Servings: 7

Ingredients:
- 8 oz chicken fillet
- ¾ cup coconut flour
- 1 egg white
- 1 teaspoon ground black pepper
- 1 teaspoon olive oil

Directions:
Cut the chicken fillet into the medium tenders. Whisk the egg whites and dip the chicken tenders into the whites. Remove the tenders from the egg white and sprinkle with the ground black pepper and coconut flour. Place the chicken tenders in the slow cooker and drizzle with the olive oil. Cook the chicken tenders for 2.5 hours. Let the cooked chicken tenders cool slightly. Serve!

Nutrition: calories 122, fat 4.4, fiber 5.2, carbs 8.8, protein 11.6

Garlic Chicken Wings

Prep time: 10 minutes | Cooking time: 6 hours | Servings: 4

Ingredients:
- 7 oz chicken wings
- 2 garlic cloves, peeled
- 1 teaspoon garlic powder
- 1 tablespoon paprika
- 2 tablespoons olive oil
- 3 tablespoons water

Directions:
Dice the garlic cloves and combine them with the paprika, garlic powder, olive oil, and water. Then place the chicken wings in the slow cooker and sprinkle with the garlic mixture. Stir the chicken wings and cook for 6 hours on Low. Chill the cooked chicken wings slightly and serve!

Nutrition: calories 164, fat 10.9, fiber 0.8, carbs 2, protein 14.8

Broccoli Balls

Prep time: 20 minutes | Cooking time: 2 hours | Servings: 4

Ingredients:
- 6 oz broccoli
- 1 egg
- 1 tablespoon almond flour
- 1 tablespoon butter
- 1 teaspoon dried parsley
- 2 oz Parmesan, grated

Directions:
Place the broccoli in a blender and blend until smooth. Beat the egg into the broccoli. Add almond flour, butter, and dried parsley. Blend the mixture for 1 minute more at maximum speed. Transfer the broccoli mixture to a big bowl. Add grated cheese and stir. Make small balls from the mix and place them in the slow cooker. Cook the broccoli balls for 2 hours on High. Serve and

Nutrition: calories 141, fat 10.7, fiber 1.9, carbs 4.9, protein 8.7

White Queso Dip

Prep time: 10 minutes | Cooking time: 4 hours | Servings: 8

Ingredients:
- 4 teaspoons butter
- 3 oz Cheddar cheese, grated
- 2 oz Monterey Jack cheese
- 2 oz full-fat cream
- 4 tablespoons water
- 1 jalapeno pepper, chopped
- 1 teaspoon minced garlic
- ¼ teaspoon salt
- 1 teaspoon ground black pepper
- ½ teaspoon dried cilantro

Directions:
Place Cheddar cheese, Monterey Jack cheese, cream, water, chopped jalapeno pepper, minced garlic, salt, and ground black pepper in the slow cooker. Add dried cilantro and butter. Cook the dip for 4 hours on Low. Stir the dip and transfer it into a bowl. Serve it!

Nutrition: calories 97, fat 8.4, fiber 0.1, carbs 0.9, protein 4.7

Keto Bread Sticks

Prep time: 25 minutes | Cooking time: 1 hour | Servings: 4

Ingredients:
- 1 egg
- 2 oz Parmesan, grated
- 1 tablespoon Psyllium husk powder
- 1 teaspoon cream cheese
- 2 tablespoons almond flour
- 1 teaspoon olive oil
- ¼ teaspoon thyme

Directions:
Beat the egg in the bowl and whisk. Add Psyllium husk powder, cream cheese, almond flour, thyme, and grated cheese. Stir the mixture until smooth and roll into medium sticks. Freeze the sticks for 10 minutes and then place them in the slow cooker. Add olive oil and cook for 1 hour on High. When the sticks are cooked, serve them hot!

Nutrition: calories 162, fat 12.6, fiber 3.3, carbs 5.7, protein 9

Cheesy Zucchini Crisps

Prep time: 10 minutes | Cooking time: 2.5 hours | Servings: 2

Ingredients:
- 2 oz zucchini, sliced
- 1 oz Parmesan, grated
- 1 teaspoon olive oil
- ½ teaspoon chili flakes

Directions:
Place the olive oil in the slow cooker. Place the zucchini slices in the slow cooker in one layer. Sprinkle the zucchini slices with chili flakes and grated Parmesan. Close the lid and cook the zucchini for 2.5 hours on High. Serve the cooked snack immediately!

Nutrition: calories 70, fat 5.4, fiber 0.3, carbs 1.5, protein 4.9

Keto Crackers

Prep time: 15 minutes | Cooking time: 2 hours | Servings: 4

Ingredients:
- 1 teaspoon butter
- ¾ cup almond flour
- ½ teaspoon salt
- 1 teaspoon ground black pepper
- 1 teaspoon cumin
- 1 teaspoon olive oil

Directions:
Mix the butter, almond flour, salt, ground black pepper, and cumin. Knead the dough until smooth Make small balls and press them gently into cracker shapes. Spray the olive oil inside the slow cooker. Add the crackers and cook for 2 hours on High. Cool the crackers and serve!

Nutrition: calories 52, fat 4.9, fiber 0.8, carbs 1.7, protein 1.3

Chia Crackers

Prep time: 20 minutes | Cooking time: 2 hours | Servings: 6

Ingredients:
- 1 tablespoon chia seeds
- 1 egg
- 1/3 cup almond flour
- 1 tablespoon coconut flour
- 1 tablespoon butter
- 1 teaspoon salt

Directions:
Beat the egg in a bowl and whisk it. Add chia seeds, almond flour, coconut flour, and salt. Knead into a dough. Toss the butter in the slow cooker. Roll out the dough and make the crackers with the help of the cutter. Place the crackers in the slow cooker cook for 2 hours on High. Cool the cooked crackers and

Nutrition: calories 64, fat5, fiber 2.3, carbs 3.2, protein 2.2

Crab Dip with Mushrooms

Prep time: 15 minutes | Cooking time: 6 hours | Servings: 4

Ingredients:
- 3 oz crab meat
- 2 oz white mushrooms, chopped
- ¼ teaspoon minced garlic
- 5 oz Cheddar cheese, shredded
- ¾ cup almond milk
- ¼ teaspoon paprika

Directions:
Chop the crab meat and place it in the slow cooker. Add the chopped mushrooms, minced garlic, shredded cheese, and almond milk. Add the paprika and stir the mixture. Cook the dip for 6 hours on Low. Then use the hand blender to puree the dip until smooth. Transfer the dip into a bowl and

Nutrition: calories 269, fat 22.9, fiber 1.2, carbs 3.9, protein 13

Artichoke Hummus

Prep time: 15 minutes | Cooking time: 6 hours | Servings: 6

Ingredients:
- 10 oz artichoke, trimmed
- 2 tablespoons butter
- 1 tablespoon olive oil
- 3 tablespoons almond milk, unsweetened
- ¼ teaspoon salt
- 1 garlic clove
- 1 teaspoon ground black pepper

Directions:
Peel the garlic clove and place it in the slow cooker. Chop the artichoke and add into the slow cooker. Add the almond milk, salt, olive oil and ground black pepper. Stir well. Cook the artichoke hummus for 6 hours on Low. Add water if you would like a softer hummus. Transfer the mixture to a blender and blend until smooth. Serve and

Nutrition: calories 95, fat 8, fiber 2.8, carbs 5.8, protein 1.8

Cauliflower Bread

Prep time: 20 minutes | Cooking time: 4 hours | Servings: 6

Ingredients:
- 7 oz cauliflower
- 1 egg, beaten
- 3 tablespoons almond flour
- ¼ teaspoon salt
- 3 tablespoons coconut flour
- 1 tablespoon Psyllium husk powder
- 1 teaspoon olive oil
- ¼ teaspoon chili flakes
- ¼ teaspoon ground black pepper

Directions:
Chop the cauliflower into tiny pieces and add the egg. Stir the mixture well and add the almond flour. Sprinkle the mixture with the salt, coconut flour, Psyllium husk powder, olive oil, chili flakes, and ground black pepper. Knead into a soft dough. Transfer the dough to a slow cooker and cook for 4 hours on High. When the bread is cooked, cool it slightly then slice.

Nutrition: calories 126, fat 8.9, fiber 8, carbs 8.7, protein 5.1

Bacon Wrapped Duck Roll

Prep time: 20 minutes | Cooking time: 3 hours | Servings: 12

Ingredients:
- 1-pound duck breast
- 5 oz bacon, sliced
- 1 teaspoon salt
- ½ teaspoon ground black pepper
- 1 teaspoon butter
- 1 teaspoon cayenne pepper
- 4 tablespoons water

Directions:
Beat the duck breast gently to flatten. Sprinkle the duck breast with the salt, ground black pepper, and cayenne pepper. Spread the butter on the duck breast and roll it. Wrap the duck breast in the bacon and put it in the slow cooker. Add the water and cook the duck roll for 3 hours on High. When the duck roll is cooked, slice it and !

Nutrition: calories 116, fat 6.8, fiber 0.1, carbs 0.3, protein 12.7

Eggplant Bacon Fries

Prep time: 15 minutes | Cooking time: 2.5 hours | Servings: 7

Ingredients:
- 6 oz bacon, sliced
- 2 eggplants
- 1 teaspoon olive oil
- ¼ teaspoon ground nutmeg
- 1 teaspoon onion powder

Directions:

Cut the eggplant into the sticks and sprinkle them with the ground nutmeg and onion powder. Toss well. Wrap the seasoned eggplant sticks in the sliced bacon. Put the bacon fries in the slow cooker and add the olive oil. Cook the bacon fries for 2.5 hours on High. Serve the cooked meal immediately!

Nutrition: calories 178, fat 11.1, fiber 5.6, carbs 9.9, protein 10.6

Mushroom Stuffed Meatballs

Prep time: 20 minutes | Cooking time: 3 hours | Servings: 4

Ingredients:
- 4 oz white mushrooms, chopped
- 1 oz Parmesan, grated
- 1 teaspoon olive oil
- 10 oz ground beef
- 1 teaspoon onion powder
- 1 tablespoon almond flour
- ½ teaspoon salt
- 1 teaspoon dried oregano

Directions:

Mix the ground beef, grated cheese, onion powder, almond flour, salt, and dried oregano and stir well. Make meatballs from the meat mixture and stuff them with the white mushrooms. Place the meatballs in the slow cooker and add olive oil. Cook the meatballs for 3 hours on High. Cool the cooked meatballs to room temperature and serve!

Nutrition: calories 214, fat 10.7, fiber 1.2, carbs 3.4, protein 26.3

Bacon Pepper Quiche

Prep time: 20 minutes | Cooking time: 4 hours | Servings: 12

Ingredients:
- 1 cup almond flour
- 3 tablespoons olive oil
- 1 teaspoon dried basil
- 1 teaspoon salt
- 4 eggs, beaten
- 1 green pepper, chopped
- 3 oz bacon, chopped
- 2 oz Parmesan, grated

Directions:

Whisk the eggs and combine them together with the dried basil, almond flour, salt, chopped green pepper, and grated cheese. Stir the mixture and add chopped bacon. Pour the olive oil in the slow cooker and add egg mixture. Cook for 4 hours on High. When the quiche is cooked, cool and slice into servings.

Nutrition: calories 120, fat 10.1, fiber 0.4, carbs 1.3, protein 6.6

Mini Muffins

Prep time: 15 minutes | Cooking time: 3 hours | Servings: 4

Ingredients:
- 4 tablespoons almond flour
- 1 egg, beaten
- 3 tablespoons coconut flour
- ¼ teaspoon baking powder
- ¼ teaspoon paprika
- 1 teaspoon butter, melted

Directions:
Whisk together the beaten egg and almond flour. Add coconut flour, baking powder, melted butter and paprika and stir until smooth. Pour the muffin mixture into mini muffin molds. Put the muffins in the slow cooker and cook for 3 hours on High. Cool the cooked muffins slightly and serve!

Nutrition: calories 207, fat 16.6, fiber 5.3, carbs 10.1, protein 8.2

Eggplant Rolls with Meat

Prep time: 25 minutes | Cooking time: 26 hours | Servings: 6

Ingredients:
- 2 eggplants
- 5 oz chicken fillet
- 1 teaspoon salt
- 1 teaspoon ground black pepper
- 3 oz Mozzarella, sliced
- 2 tablespoons butter

Directions:
Slice the eggplant lengthwise. Mix the salt and ground black pepper. Chop the chicken fillet and sprinkle it with the spices. Place a small amount of the meat mix on each of the eggplant slices. Roll the eggplant slices, enclosing the meat, and secure with a toothpick. Place the eggplant rolls in the slow cooker and add water and butter. Cook the rolls for 6 hours. Chill the eggplant rolls slightly. Serve!

Nutrition: calories 165, fat 8.4, fiber 6.5, carbs 11.5, protein 12.7

Desserts

Keto Chocolate Bars

Prep time: 20 minutes | Cooking time: 3 hours | Servings: 8

Ingredients:
- 1 oz dark chocolate
- 1 tablespoons chia seeds
- 1 cup almond flour
- 1 egg, beaten
- 1 tablespoons liquid stevia
- 1 teaspoon vanilla extract
- ½ cup almond milk, unsweetened

Directions:

Melt the dark chocolate and mix it with the beaten egg. Whisk the mixture until smooth. Add the liquid stevia, vanilla extract, and almond milk. Whisk the mixture until smooth. Add almond flour and stir the dough with a spatula. When the dough is smooth, add the chia seeds and stir it well. Transfer the dough to the slow cooker and flatten it gently. Close the lid and cook the dessert for 3 hours on High or until the bar is set in the middle. Let the cooked dessert cool. Cut into bars and place on a serving platter. Serve!

Nutrition: calories 100, fat 8, fiber 2.1, carbs 5.3, protein 2.6

Keto Cobbler

Prep time: 15 minutes | Cooking time: 2 hours | Servings: 4

Ingredients:
- 1 cup blackberries
- 1 tablespoon liquid stevia
- 1 teaspoon Psyllium Husk
- 5 tablespoons almond flour
- 1 egg, beaten
- 1 tablespoon butter

Directions:

Whisk the egg and combine them with the almond flour and Psyllium Husk. Add the liquid stevia and butter and knead into a smooth dough. Chop the dough into small pieces. Cover the bottom of the slow cooker with parchment. Place a small amount of the dough in the bottom of the slow cooker. Sprinkle the dough with a small amount of the blackberries. Add a second layer of the chopped dough followed by more blackberries. Continue layering until you use all the ingredients. Close the lid and cook the cobbler for 2 hours on High. Let the cooked cobbler cool slightly. Serve it!

Nutrition: calories 264, fat 21.7, fiber 8, carbs 13.9, protein 9.4

Soft Bacon Cookies

Prep time: 25 minutes | Cooking time: 3 hours | Servings: 6

Ingredients:
- ½ cup almond flour
- 1 egg, beaten
- 3 tablespoons butter, melted
- 3 oz bacon, chopped cooked
- 1 teaspoon olive oil
- 1 teaspoon stevia extract

Directions:
Whisk the egg and mix it with the butter and olive oil. Add the stevia extract and stir the mixture gently. Add the almond flour and knead the dough. When the dough is smooth, add the chopped bacon and knead it again. Make medium cookies by rolling the dough into small balls with your hands. Place the cookies in the slow cooker and cook for 3 hours on Low. Check if the cookies are cooked and remove them from the slow cooker. Cool slightly. Serve!

Nutrition: calories 198, fat 17.9, fiber 1, carbs 2.3, protein 8.2

Keto Brownies

Prep time: 20 minutes | Cooking time: 3 hours | Servings: 8

Ingredients:
- 1 teaspoon baking soda
- 1 oz dark chocolate
- 2 teaspoons liquid stevia
- 1 teaspoon vanilla extract
- 1 teaspoon ground cinnamon
- 1 cup almond flour
- 3 tablespoons butter, melted
- 1 egg, beaten
- 1 tablespoon full-fat cream

Directions:
Melt the chocolate and mix it with the liquid stevia vanilla extract and ground cinnamon. Add the butter and almond flour. Add the egg and cream. Stir the mixture until smooth. Transfer the mixture to the slow cooker. Flatten it gently and cook for 3 hours on High. Cut the cooked dessert into the servings.

Nutrition: calories 43, fat 3, fiber 0.3, carbs 2.6, protein 1.3

Keto Peanut Butter Cookies

Prep time: 20 minutes | Cooking time: 2 hours | Servings: 6

Ingredients:
- 4 tablespoons peanut butter, unsweetened
- 4 tablespoons almond flour
- 1 teaspoon vanilla extract
- 1 teaspoon liquid stevia
- 1 tablespoon coconut flakes, unsweetened

Directions:
Mix the peanut butter, almond flour, vanilla extract, and liquid stevia. Mix until smooth. Knead the dough with the coconut flakes. Make the small balls from the dough and flatten them gently. Place the cookies in the slow cooker and cook them for 2 hours on High. Chill the cooked cookies and store them in the paper bags to prevent them from drying out.

Nutrition: calories 174, fat 15, fiber 2.7, carbs 6.3, protein 6.7

Mint Pudding

Prep time: 10 minutes | Cooking time: 3 hours | Servings: 4

Ingredients:
- 1 teaspoon dried mint
- 1 teaspoon xanthan gum
- 1 egg yolk
- 1 tablespoon Erythritol
- 1 cup full-fat cream
- 1 teaspoon vanilla extract
- 1 tablespoon whipped cream

Directions:
Whisk the egg yolk and combine it with the dried mint, xanthan gum, Erythritol, cream, and vanilla extract. Whisk the mixture until smooth. Place the mixture in the slow cooker and add whipped cream. Cook the pudding for 3 hours on Low. When the pudding is cooked, serve it immediately!

Nutrition: calories 61, fat 5.4, fiber 0, carbs 2.2, protein 0.8

Keto Chip Cookies

Prep time: 15 minutes | Cooking time: 2.5 hours | Servings: 7

Ingredients:
- 1 cup almond flour
- 4 tablespoons butter, melted
- 2 tablespoons Erythritol
- 1 egg, beaten
- 2 tablespoons sugar-free chocolate chips
- 1 teaspoon vanilla extract

Directions:
Mix the beaten egg and butter. Add the vanilla extract and almond flour. Stir the mixture well and add Erythritol. Mix well and add chocolate chips. Knead the dough and divide into small cookies. Place the cookies in the slow cooker and cook for 2.5 hours on High. Let the cooked cookies cool slightly.

Nutrition: calories 92, fat 9.2, fiber 0.4, carbs 5.3, protein 1.7

Coconut Bars

Prep time: 10 minutes | Cooking time: 2 hours | Servings: 8

Ingredients:
- 1 cup coconut flour
- 2 tablespoons coconut flakes, unsweetened
- 3 tablespoons butter
- 1 egg, beaten
- 1 teaspoon baking powder
- 1 teaspoon vanilla extract

Directions:
Mix the coconut flour and coconut flakes. Add the butter and beaten egg. Add baking powder and vanilla extract. Stir the dough until smooth. Place the dough in the slow cooker, press down to flatten and cook it for 2 hours on High. Cut the dessert into the bars and serve!

Nutrition: calories 113, fat 6.8, fiber 6.1, carbs 10.6, protein 2.8

Spoon Cake

Prep time: 15 minutes | Cooking time: 2 hours | Servings: 6

Ingredients:
- ½ cup almond milk, unsweetened
- 1 teaspoon baking powder
- 1 cup almond flour
- 1 tablespoon butter
- 1 oz dark chocolate
- 2 tablespoons Erythritol
- 1 teaspoon ground cinnamon

Directions:
Mix the baking powder, almond milk, almond flour, butter, Erythritol, and ground cinnamon. Chop the chocolate. Stir the flour mixture until smooth, add the chopped chocolate. Stir and transfer in the slow cooker. Cook the cake for 2 hours on High. Let the cake cool for 10 minutes and serve!

Nutrition: calories 117, fat 10.4, fiber 1.3, carbs 9.6, protein 1.9

Sweet Bacon Slices

Prep time: 10 minutes | Cooking time: 2 hours | Servings: 2

Ingredients:
- 4 bacon slices
- 1 tablespoon Erythritol
- 1 tablespoon butter
- ¼ teaspoon ground cinnamon

Directions:
Melt the butter and combine it with the ground cinnamon and Erythritol. Place the sliced bacon in the slow cooker and brush it with the butter mixture. Close the lid and cook the bacon for 2 hours on High. Let the cooked bacon cool slightly.

Nutrition: calories 257, fat 21.6, fiber 0.2, carbs 8.3, protein 14.2

Pound Cake

Prep time: 15 minutes | Cooking time: 3 hours | Servings: 8

Ingredients:
- 1 cup almond flour
- ¼ cup coconut flour
- 1 teaspoon vanilla extract
- 3 tablespoons butter
- 2 egg, beaten
- 1 teaspoon baking powder
- 2 teaspoons full-fat cream cheese

Directions:
Whisk the eggs and combine them with the baking powder and cream cheese. Stir and add vanilla extract and coconut flour. Add the almond flour and stir the mixture until smooth. Place the cake in the slow cooker and cook for 3 hours on High. Cool the cooked cake and cut into the servings.

Nutrition: calories 92, fat 7.6, fiber 1.9, carbs 3.8, protein 2.9

Sweet Sesame Buns

Prep time: 20 minutes | Cooking time: 3 hours | Servings: 8

Ingredients:
- 1 tablespoon sesame seeds
- 2 tablespoons butter
- 1 egg, beaten
- 1 egg white
- 1 cup almond flour
- 1 tablespoon coconut flakes, sesame
- ¼ cup Erythritol
- 1 teaspoon vanilla extract

Directions:
Whisk the egg and egg whites. Add the butter and almond flour. Add Erythritol, vanilla and coconut flakes and knead into a smooth dough. Form small buns from the dough and place them in the slow cooker. Sprinkle the buns with the sesame seeds and cook for 3 hours on High. Cool the cooked buns until room temperature and transfer onto a platter.

Nutrition: calories 66, fat 6, fiber 0.6, carbs 20.8, protein 2.1

Almond Cookies

Prep time: 15 minutes | Cooking time: 2 hours | Servings: 6

Ingredients:
- 1 oz almonds, chopped
- 3 tablespoons butter
- ½ cup almond flour
- 1 teaspoon vanilla extract
- 1 teaspoon baking powder
- 2 tablespoons Erythritol

Directions:
Combine the almond flour, vanilla extract, baking powder, and Erythritol. Stir the mixture and add butter. Knead into a smooth dough. Make small balls from the dough and sprinkle the balls with the almonds. Press the almond into the cookies gently. Transfer the cookies to the slow cooker. Cook the cookies for 2 hours on High. Cool the cookies.

Nutrition: calories 94, fat 9.3, fiber 0.9, carbs7, protein 1.6

Avocado Muffins

Prep time: 15 minutes | Cooking time: 2.5hours | Servings: 4

Ingredients:
- 1 egg, beaten
- 1 teaspoon baking powder
- 1 avocado, mashed
- 3 tablespoons almond flour
- 1 tablespoon butter
- 2 teaspoons liquid stevia
- 1 teaspoon coconut flour

Directions:
Whisk together the egg and mashed avocado. Add the baking powder and almond flour. Add the butter and liquid stevia. Sprinkle the mixture with the coconut flour and knead the dough. Place the dough in 4 muffin molds. Transfer the muffins to the slow cooker and cook for 2.5 hours on High. Cool the cooked muffins and serve!

Nutrition: calories 265, fat 24.3, fiber 5.7, carbs 9.5, protein 6.9

Walnut Balls

Prep time: 15 minutes | Cooking time: 2.5 hours | Servings: 6

Ingredients:
- 2 oz walnuts, chopped
- 4 tablespoons butter
- 1 teaspoon baking powder
- 1 tablespoon Erythritol
- 4 tablespoons almond flour
- 1 teaspoon liquid stevia
- 1 egg, beaten

Directions:
Mix the chopped walnuts and butter. Add baking powder and Erythritol. Add almond flour, liquid stevia, and egg. Knead the dough until smooth. Make small balls from the dough. Cover the bottom of the slow cooker with the parchment and place the walnut balls inside. Cook the dessert for 2.5 hours on High. When the walnut balls are cooked, serve them immediately!

Nutrition: calories 166, fat 16.2, fiber 1.2, carbs 4.9, protein 4.3

Rhubarb Crumble

Prep time: 15 minutes | Cooking time: 3 hours | Servings: 8

Ingredients:
- 8 oz rhubarb, chopped
- 1/3 cup Erythritol
- 1 teaspoon vanilla extract
- ½ cup almond flour
- 4 tablespoons butter
- 2 oz walnuts, chopped

Directions:
Mix the vanilla extract, almond flour, and butter. Add walnuts and knead the dough. Chop the dough into small pieces. Cover the bottom of the slow cooker with parchment. Sprinkle it with the small amount of the chopped dough. Add some of the rhubarb and sprinkle it with some Erythritol. Add a layer of the dough again and repeat all the steps until you finish all the ingredients. Cook the crumble for 3 hours on High. Cool the crumble and serve!

Nutrition: calories 112, fat 10.9, fiber 1.2, carbs 12.4, protein 2.4

Blueberry Pie

Prep time: 15 minutes | Cooking time: 4 hours | Servings: 8

Ingredients:
- 2 oz blueberry
- 1 cup almond flour
- 1 cup almond milk, unsweetened
- 1 teaspoon baking powder
- ¼ cup Erythritol
- 1 teaspoon butter
- 1 teaspoon vanilla extract

Directions:
Mix the almond flour and almond milk. Add baking powder and Erythritol and stir. Add the butter and vanilla extract and stir until smooth. Place the dough in the slow cooker. Add the blueberries and flatten the pie gently. Close the lid and cook the pie for 4 hours on High. Cool the pie and cut into the servings.

Nutrition: calories 99, fat 9.4, fiber 1.2, carbs 11.3, protein 1.5

Sesame Cookies

Prep time: 20 minutes | Cooking time: 2 hours | Servings: 4

Ingredients:
- 2 tablespoons coconut flour
- 1 tablespoon butter
- 1 tablespoon sesame seeds
- ½ teaspoon baking powder
- 1 egg
- 1 teaspoon vanilla extract

Directions:
Mix the coconut flour and butter. Add the baking soda and vanilla extract. Beat the eggs into the mixture. Add the sesame seeds and knead the dough. Roll out the dough and cut out cookies with a cookie cutter. Place the cookies in the slow cooker and cook them for 2 hours on High. Chill the cookies and serve!

Nutrition: calories 73, fat 5.5, fiber 1.8, carbs 3.5, protein 2.3

Keto Soufflé

Prep time: 15 minutes | Cooking time: 2.5 hours | Servings: 5

Ingredients:
- 1 tablespoon butter
- ¼ cup Erythritol
- 1 oz dark chocolate
- 4 egg yolks
- 2 egg whites
- 5 teaspoon whipped cream

Directions:
Whisk the butter with Erythritol. Add the egg yolks and stir until well blended. Whisk the eggs to stiff peaks. Melt the chocolate and combine it with the egg yolk mixture. Add the egg whites and whipped cream. Stir gently to get a smooth batter. Place the mixture in ramekins and put the ramekins in the slow cooker. Cook the soufflé for 2.5 hours on Low. Serve it immediately!

Nutrition: calories 115, fat 9.2, fiber 0.2, carbs 16.1, protein 4.2

Sweet Zucchini Muffins

Prep time: 10 minutes | Cooking time: 3 hours | Servings: 6

Ingredients:
- 2 oz zucchini, grated
- 1 teaspoon baking powder
- 1 teaspoon vanilla extract
- 3 teaspoons Erythritol
- 1 cup almond flour
- 3 tablespoons butter
- 1 tablespoon almond milk, unsweetened

Directions:
Mix all the ingredients together. Stir them well to get a smooth batter. Place the muffins in the muffin molds and transfer them to the slow cooker. Cook the muffins for 3 hours on High. When the muffins are cooked cool slightly.

Nutrition: calories 88, fat 8.7, fiber 0.7, carbs 4.4, protein 1.2

Chocolate Mousse

Prep time: 20 minutes | Cooking time: 4 hours | Servings: 4

Ingredients:
- 2 oz dark chocolate
- 2 egg whites
- 1 cup almond milk, unsweetened
- 1 tablespoon full-fat cream cheese

Directions:
Melt the chocolate and combine it with the almond milk. Whisk the egg whites until soft peaks and combine it together with the cream cheese. Whisk it gently for 1 minute more. Combine chocolate mixture and egg white mixture. Stir and transfer into ramekins. Place the ramekins in the slow cooker and cook on Low for 4 hours. Serve the cooked mousse!

Nutrition: calories 231, fat 6.719.4, fiber 1.8, carbs 11.9, protein 4.4

Keto Truffles

Prep time: 15 minutes | Cooking time: 2 hours | Servings: 5

Ingredients:
- 2 tablespoons cocoa powder
- 1 tablespoon Erythritol
- 1 oz dark chocolate
- 2 tablespoons butter
- 3 tablespoon almond flour
- 1 tablespoon coconut flour
- 1 egg, beaten

Directions:
Mix the Erythritol, butter, almond flour, and coconut flour. Add the beaten egg and stir until smooth. Melt the chocolate and add it to the flour mixture. Knead until smooth. Make small balls from the dough and coat them in the cocoa powder. Place the truffles in the slow cooker and cook for 2 hours on High. Cool truffles and serve!

Nutrition: calories 190, fat 16, fiber 3.2, carbs 12.2, protein 5.8

Coconut Bars

Prep time: 15 minutes | Cooking time: 3 hours | Servings: 7

Ingredients:
- ¼ cup coconut flakes, unsweetened
- 1 cup coconut flour
- ½ cup almond milk, unsweetened
- 1 teaspoon baking powder
- 1 teaspoon vanilla extract
- 1 teaspoon butter

Directions:
Mix the coconut flakes and coconut flour. Add the baking soda and stir the mixture. Add the butter and vanilla extract. Add the almond milk and stir it until smooth. Transfer the mixture to the slow cooker. Flatten it with a spatula and cook for 3 hours on High. Cut the cooked dessert into bars and serve!

Nutrition: calories 125, fat 7.3, fiber 7.5, carbs 13.2, protein 2.8

Candied Almonds

Prep time: 10 minutes | Cooking time: 3 hours | Servings: 6

Ingredients:
- 1 cup almonds
- 1/3 cup granulated monk fruit sweetener
- 4 tablespoons water
- ¼ teaspoon ground cinnamon

Directions:

Mix the sweetener and water. Add the ground cinnamon and stir. Place the almonds in the slow cooker. Add the sweetener mix and stir. Cook the almonds for 3 hours on High. Cool the dessert a little.

Nutrition: calories 92, fat 7.9, fiber 2, carbs 3.5, protein 3.4

Vanilla Cream

Prep time: 15 minutes | Cooking time: 2 hours | Servings: 6

Ingredients:
- 2 egg whites
- 4 tablespoons Erythritol
- 1 teaspoon vanilla extract
- 1 cup almond milk, unsweetened
- 1 teaspoon ground cinnamon
- ½ teaspoon turmeric

Directions:

Whisk the egg whites until soft peaks and add Erythritol. Add the vanilla extract and almond milk. Keep whisking the mixture for 2 minutes more. Then add the ground cinnamon and turmeric. Stir the mixture gently and transfer to the slow cooker. Cook the cream for 2 hours on Low. Transfer the cooked dessert into ramekins and

Nutrition: calories 101, fat 9.6, fiber 1.1, carbs 12.8, protein 2.2

Snowball Cookies

Prep time: 20 minutes | Cooking time: 2.5 hours | Servings: 6

Ingredients:
- 2 tablespoons coconut flakes, unsweetened
- 1 egg, beaten
- 4 tablespoons flour
- 2 tablespoons butter
- 1 tablespoon Erythritol
- 1 tablespoon water

Directions:

Mix the egg, flour, butter, Erythritol, and water. Knead into a smooth dough. Make small balls from the dough and coat them in the coconut flakes. Place the cookies in the slow cooker and cook for 2.5 hours on High. Chill the cookies and serve!

Nutrition: calories 69, fat 5.2, fiber 0.3, carbs 6.8, protein 1.6

Dessert Pancakes

Prep time: 10 minutes | Cooking time: 2 hours | Servings: 2

Ingredients:

- ¼ cup almond milk, unsweetened
- 1 teaspoon vanilla extract
- 1 teaspoon ground cinnamon
- 1 teaspoon baking powder
- 1 cup almond flour
- 1 egg, beaten
- 1 tablespoon butter
- 1 teaspoon olive oil

Directions:

Whisk the egg and combine it with the almond milk, vanilla extract, ground cinnamon, baking powder, and almond flour. Add the butter and stir it until smooth. Spray the slow cooker with the olive oil. Pour the pancake batter into the slow cooker and cook for 2 hours on High. Cut the pancake into servings!

Nutrition: calories 263, fat 24.5, fiber 2.8, carbs 7.2, protein 6.6

Cinnamon Cup Cake

Prep time: 15 minutes | Cooking time: 3 hours | Servings: 6

Ingredients:

- 1 teaspoon ground cinnamon
- 2 eggs
- 1 cup almond milk, unsweetened
- ½ cup coconut flour
- ½ teaspoon baking soda
- 2 tablespoon stevia extract
- 1 oz walnuts, chopped

Directions:

Beat the eggs in a big bowl and whisk well. Add ground cinnamon and almond milk and stir gently. Then add baking soda and stevia extract. Whisk the mixture until smooth and add chopped walnuts. Stir the batter and place it in small ramekins. Put the ramekins in the slow cooker and cook for 3 hours on High.

Nutrition: calories 183, fat 14.8, fiber 5.4, carbs 9.8, protein 5.3

Pudding Cake

Prep time: 25 minutes | Cooking time: 3 hours | Servings: 6

Ingredients:

- 2 tablespoons butter
- 1 oz dark chocolate
- 2 oz full-fat cream
- 1 teaspoon vanilla extract
- 1 tablespoon cocoa powder
- 4 tablespoons coconut flour
- 3 eggs, beaten
- 3 tablespoons Erythritol
- 1 teaspoon olive oil

Directions:

Melt the duck chocolate and combine it with the butter, cream, and vanilla extract. Stir the mixture until smooth. Add the cocoa powder and coconut flour. Add the beaten eggs and Erythritol. Whisk the mixture until smooth. Transfer the cake mixture to the slow cooker. Cook for 3 hours on High. Serve the cooked cake after 10 minutes of chilling!

Nutrition: calories 146, fat 10.9, fiber 2.4, carbs 15.6, protein 4.3

Keto Fudge

Prep time: 15 minutes | Cooking time: 3 hours | Servings: 12

Ingredients:
- 5 tablespoons butter
- 1 oz dark chocolate
- 3 tablespoons almond flour
- ½ cup Erythritol
- 1 teaspoon vanilla extract
- 4 tablespoons cocoa powder
- 1 tablespoon cream cheese

Directions:
Combine the butter and dark chocolate and preheat the mixture. When the mixture is melted, add the almond flour, Erythritol, vanilla extract, and cocoa powder. Add the cream cheese and stir. Place the fudge mixture in the slow cooker and cook it for 3 hours on High. Serve the cooked fudge hot!

Nutrition: calories 103, fat 9.5, fiber 1.4, carbs 14 protein 2.1

Kombucha Cake

Prep time: 25 minutes | Cooking time: 3 hours | Servings: 8

Ingredients:
- 1 cup almond flour
- ¼ cup coconut flour
- 2 tablespoons Erythritol
- ¼ teaspoon baking powder
- 3 eggs, beaten
- 2 tablespoons kombucha
- ¾ teaspoon salt

Directions:
Mix the almond flour and coconut flour. Add the Erythritol and baking powder. Add the kombucha and salt and stir the mixture. Add the beaten eggs and stir the batter until smooth. Place the batter in the slow cooker and cook for 3 hours on High. Chill the cooked cake slightly.

Nutrition: calories 59, fat 3.8, fiber 1.9, carbs 7.2, protein 3.3

Gingerbread Cookies

Prep time: 20 minutes | Cooking time: 2.5 hours | Servings: 6

Ingredients:
- 1 teaspoon ground ginger
- 1 teaspoon ground cinnamon
- 1 teaspoon vanilla extract
- 1 cup almond flour
- 4 tablespoons butter
- 1 egg, whisked
- 1 teaspoon baking powder

Directions:
Add the ground ginger, ground cinnamon, vanilla extract, almond flour, and baking powder into a large bowl. Stir and add the butter and whisked the egg. Knead into a soft dough. Roll it out with a rolling pin and make the cookies. Place the cookies in the slow cooker and cook them for 2.5 hours on High. Chill the cookies and serve!

Nutrition: calories195, fat 17.3, fiber 2.3, carbs 5.1, protein 5.1

Chewy Seed and Nut Bars

Prep time: 15 minutes | Cooking time: 1 hour | Servings: 6

Ingredients:
- 2 tablespoons swerve
- 1 tablespoon Erythritol
- 1 oz pumpkin seeds
- 1 oz almonds, chopped
- 1 tablespoon butter
- 2 tablespoons flour
- 1 teaspoon coconut flakes, unsweetened

Directions:
Mix the swerve, Erythritol, pumpkin seeds, almond, butter, flour, and coconut flakes. Stir the mix well. Place it in the slow cooker and flatten the surface. Cook the dessert for 1 hour on High. Let the bars cool slightly. Cut it into the bars and serve!

Nutrition: calories 82, fat 6.6, fiber 0.9, carbs 7, protein 2.5

Red Velvet Cupcakes

Prep time: 20 minutes | Cooking time: 3 hours | Servings: 6

Ingredients:
- 1 cup almond flour
- 3 eggs
- 3 tablespoons butter
- 1 teaspoon baking powder
- 1 teaspoon vanilla extract
- ¼ cup full-fat whipped cream
- 3 tablespoons Erythritol
- Red food coloring

Directions:
Beat the eggs in a bowl and whisk well. Add butter, baking powder, vanilla extract, and whipped cream. Add Erythritol and food coloring. Stir the mixture until well blended and add almond flour. Stir until smooth. Place the mixture in the muffin molds and transfer them to the slow cooker. Cook for 3 hours on High. Cool the cupcakes and serve!

Nutrition: calories 114, fat 10.3, fiber 0.5, carbs 9.5, protein 3.8

Keto Cheesecake

Prep time: 20 minutes | Cooking time: 6 hours | Servings: 6

Ingredients:
- 3 tablespoons butter
- 3 tablespoons almond flour
- ½ teaspoon ground cinnamon
- 1 tablespoons liquid stevia
- 6 oz full-fat cream cheese
- 1 teaspoon vanilla extract
- 1 tablespoon full-fat cream
- 3 tablespoons Erythritol
- 2 eggs, whisked

Directions:
Mix the butter, almond flour, and ground cinnamon. Add the liquid stevia, cream cheese, and vanilla extract and stir well. Add the cream and Erythritol. Add the whisked eggs and stir it well. Pour 1 cup of water in the slow cooker. Transfer the batter into a cheesecake mold. Place the cheesecake mold in the slow cooker and cook it for 6 hours on Low. Cool the cooked cheesecake a little. Serve it!

Nutrition: calories 195, fat 19, fiber 0.5, carbs 1.9, protein 4.9

Lavender Cookies

Prep time: 15 minutes | Cooking time: 2 hours | Servings: 6

Ingredients:
- 1 teaspoon lavender extract
- 1 teaspoon vanilla extract
- 1 cup coconut flour
- ¼ cup butter
- 1 egg, whisked
- 1 teaspoon baking powder
- ½ teaspoon olive oil

Directions:

Mix the lavender extract and vanilla extract. Add the coconut flour and butter. Add the whisked egg and baking powder. Knead into a smooth dough. Roll out the dough and cut the cookies with a cookie cutter. Pour the olive oil in the slow cooker. Transfer the cookies to the slow cooker and cook them for 2 hours on High. Cool the cookies and serve!

Nutrition: calories 165, fat 10.8, fiber 8, carbs 13.9, protein 3.7

Mini Pumpkin Cakes

Prep time: 15 minutes | Cooking time: 6 hours | Servings: 8

Ingredients:
- 2 oz pumpkin puree
- 6 tablespoons almond flour
- ½ teaspoon baking soda
- 1 teaspoon ground cinnamon
- ¼ teaspoon ground cardamom
- 1 teaspoon vanilla extract
- ¾ cup almond milk, unsweetened
- 1 tablespoon butter
- 1 oz walnuts, chopped

Directions:

Combine the pumpkin puree, almond flour, and baking soda. Add the ground cinnamon, ground cardamom, and vanilla extract. Stir the mixture gently and add almond milk and butter. Add the chopped walnuts and stir the batter until smooth. Place the mixture into small cake molds and transfer them to a slow cooker. Cook the cakes for 6 hours on Low. Cool the cakes slightly and serve!

Nutrition: calories 211, fat 19.4, fiber 3.4, carbs 7, protein 6

Walnut Muffins

Prep time: 15 minutes | Cooking time: 3 hours | Servings: 8

Ingredients:
- 2 oz walnuts, chopped
- 5 tablespoons butter
- 1 cup coconut flour
- 1 teaspoon vanilla extract
- 1 egg
- 2 tablespoons liquid stevia
- 3 tablespoons almond milk, unsweetened
- 1 teaspoon baking powder

Directions:
Mix the butter, flour, vanilla extract, liquid stevia, almond milk, and baking powder. Beat the egg into the mixture and whisk it well until smooth. Add the chopped walnuts and stir well. Place the dough in the muffin molds and transfer into the slow cooker. Cook the muffins for 3 hours on High. Cool the cooked muffins and

Nutrition: calories 190, fat 14.8, fiber 6.6, carbs 11.4, protein 4.6

Vanilla Rolls

Prep time: 20 minutes | Cooking time: 3 hours | Servings: 8

Ingredients:
- 1 tablespoon vanilla extract
- 3 tablespoons Erythritol
- ½ cup almond milk, unsweetened
- 1 cup almond flour
- 1 tablespoon cocoa powder
- 1 tablespoon coconut flour
- 1 teaspoon butter

Directions:
Mix the butter, coconut flour, cocoa powder, almond flour, almond milk, and vanilla extract. Add the Erythritol and knead into a smooth dough. Roll out the dough it into a log. Cut the log into slices and place them in the slow cooker. Cook the vanilla rolls for 3 hours on High. Chill the rolls to room temperature and serve!

Nutrition: calories 69, fat 6, fiber 1.3, carbs 8.4, protein 1.4

Cinnamon Swirls

Prep time: 20 minutes | Cooking time: 3 hours | Servings: 8

Ingredients:
- 1 teaspoon baking powder
- 1 cup almond flour
- 1/3 cup butter
- 1 tablespoon ground cinnamon
- 1 teaspoon vanilla extract
- 3 tablespoons Erythritol

Directions:
Combine the butter and almond flour. Add Erythritol and baking powder. Add vanilla extract and knead the dough. Roll out the dough and sprinkle it with the ground cinnamon. Then roll the dough into a spiral and cut into thick swirls. Place the swirls in the slow cooker and cook for 3 hours. Chill the swirls and serve!

Nutrition: calories 92, fat 9.4, fiber 0.8, carbs 9, protein 0.9

Lava Cake

Prep time: 10 minutes | Cooking time: 2.5 hours | Servings: 6

Ingredients:
- 1 oz dark chocolate
- 1 tablespoon cocoa powder
- 6 tablespoons almond flour
- ¼ cup almond milk, unsweetened
- 3 tablespoons liquid stevia

Directions:
Combine the cocoa powder and almond flour. Add almond milk and liquid stevia. Stir the mixture until smooth. Place the batter in ramekins and place the dark chocolate in the center of the cake. Cook the lava cake for 2.5 hours on High. Serve the cake immediately while hot!

Nutrition: calories 210, fat 17.9, fiber 3.7, carbs 9.8, protein 6.

Keto Sweet Bread

Prep time: 15 minutes | Cooking time: 4 hours | Servings: 8

Ingredients:
- 1 cup coconut flour
- ¼ cup Erythritol
- 1 teaspoon baking powder
- ¼ cup almond milk
- 3 tablespoons butter
- 1 oz pumpkin seeds

Directions:
Mix the coconut flour and Erythritol. Add the baking powder and almond milk. Add butter and stir it gently. Add the pumpkin seeds and knead the dough. Place the dough in the slow cooker and cook the bread for 4 hours on High. Slice the cooked bread and

Nutrition: calories 135, fat 9.2, fiber 6.3, carbs 18.9, protein 3.1

Avocado Bars

Prep time: 15 minutes | Cooking time: 3 hours | Servings: 6

Ingredients:
- 1 avocado, pitted
- ¾ cup coconut flour
- 1 teaspoon vanilla extract
- 4 tablespoons butter
- 2 tablespoons liquid stevia
- 3 tablespoons almond flour
- ½ teaspoon baking powder

Directions:
Peel the avocado and mash it. Combine the mashed avocado and coconut flour. Add vanilla extract and butter. After this, add liquid stevia, baking powder and almond flour. Stir the mix until smooth and transfer in the slow cooker. Flatten it gently and cook for 3 hours on High. Cut the cooked dessert into bars and serve!

Nutrition: calories 174, fat15.1, fiber 5.8, carbs 6, protein 1.9

Raspberry Tart
Prep time: 20 minutes | Cooking time: 4 hours | Servings: 6
Ingredients:
- 1 cup raspberries
- 4 tablespoons coconut flour
- 4 tablespoons butter
- 3 tablespoons Erythritol
- 1 teaspoon vanilla extract
- 1 teaspoon ground ginger

Directions:
Combine butter, coconut flour, ground ginger, and vanilla extract. Knead the dough. Cover the bottom of the slow cooker with parchment. Place the dough in the slow cooker and flatten it to the shape of a pie crust. Place the raspberries over the piecrust and sprinkle with Erythritol. Cook the tart for 4 hours on High. Serve the cooked tart chilled.

Nutrition: calories 101, fat 7.9, fiber 1.5, carbs 14.2, protein 0.9

Rhubarb Bars
Prep time: 15 minutes | Cooking time: 3 hours | Servings: 4
Ingredients:
- 5 oz rhubarb, chopped
- 2 tablespoons liquid stevia
- 1 teaspoon swerve
- 1 teaspoon vanilla extract
- 4 tablespoons butter
- 4 tablespoons coconut flour
- ¼ teaspoon ground cinnamon

Directions:
Combine the liquid stevia, swerve, vanilla extract, butter, coconut flour, and ground cinnamon. Knead into a smooth dough. Place the dough in the slow cooker and flatten it into the shape of a pie crust. Sprinkle with the chopped rhubarb and press gently. Close the lid and cook the dessert for 3 hours. Cool and cut into the bars.

Nutrition: calories 42, fat 0.8, fiber 3.7, carbs 7.4, protein 1.3

Pecan Cookies
Prep time: 15 minutes | Cooking time: 3 hours | Servings: 7
Ingredients:
- 2 oz pecans, chopped
- 1 cup almond flour
- 1/3 cup almond milk, unsweetened
- ½ teaspoon baking powder
- 1 teaspoon vanilla extract
- 1 teaspoon cocoa powder
- 1 tablespoons Erythritol

Directions:
Combine the almond flour and almond milk. Add the baking powder and vanilla extract. Add the cocoa powder and Erythritol. Knead the dough and cut into pieces. Roll the dough into balls and press them gently to flatten. Press the pecans inside the center of the cookies and put them in the slow cooker. Cook the cookies for 3 hours on High.

Nutrition: calories 108, fat 10.5, fiber 1.6 carbs 5.2, protein 2

Flax Seeds Balls

Prep time: 15 minutes | Cooking time: 2.5 hours | Servings: 4

Ingredients:
- 4 teaspoons flax seeds
- 2 tablespoons almond flour
- 1 tablespoon butter
- 1 tablespoon liquid stevia
- 1 teaspoon coconut flakes, unsweetened

Directions:
Combine all the ingredients in a mixing bowl. Knead the dough and then divide into small balls. Place the balls in the slow cooker and cook for 2.5 hours on High. Chill the cooked balls and serve!

Nutrition: calories 119, fat 10.8, fiber 2.2, carbs 3.7, protein 3.5

Sunflower Seeds Cookies

Prep time: 10 minutes | Cooking time: 3 hours | Servings: 10

Ingredients:
- 3 oz sunflower seeds
- 6 tablespoons butter
- 2 tablespoons liquid stevia
- 10 tablespoons almond flour
- 1 teaspoon baking powder
- 1 teaspoon vanilla extract
- 1 teaspoon cocoa powder
- ¼ teaspoon ground cardamom

Directions:
Combine the sunflower seeds, butter, liquid stevia, almond flour, baking powder, vanilla extract, cocoa powder, and ground cardamom. Knead into a smooth dough and make small cookies. Put the cookies in the slow cooker and cook for 3 hours on High. Chill the cookies well and serve!

Nutrition: calories 273, fat 25.3, fiber 3.8, carbs 8.1, protein 7.9

Tender Lime Cake

Prep time: 15 minutes | Cooking time: 4 hours | Servings: 12

Ingredients:
- 1 lime, sliced
- 1 cup almond milk, unsweetened
- 1 ½ cup coconut flour
- 1 teaspoon vanilla extract
- 1 teaspoon baking powder
- 3 tablespoons Erythritol

Directions:
Combine the almond milk, coconut flour, vanilla extract, baking powder, and Erythritol. Add the vanilla extract and stir until smooth. Place the mixture in the slow cooker. Then place the sliced lime over the cake. Cook for 4 hours on High. Check if the cake is cooked and chill. Slice the cake into servings and

Nutrition: calories 109, fat 6.3, fiber 6.6, carbs 8, protein 2.

Keto Almond Scones

Prep time: 25 minutes | Cooking time: 4 hours | Servings: 4

Ingredients:
- ½ teaspoon baking soda
- ½ cup almond flour
- ¼ cup coconut milk
- 2 eggs, beaten
- 1 teaspoon vanilla extract
- 3 tablespoons coconut flour
- 1 oz almonds, chopped

Directions:

Combine the baking soda and almond flour. Add the coconut milk and beaten eggs, Add the vanilla extract and stir the mixture gently. Add the coconut flour and almonds. Stir the mixture and knead into a dough. Make into small scones and put them in the slow cooker. Cook the scones for 4 hours on High. Chill the cooked scones and then remove them from the slow cooker to col slightly.

Nutrition: calories 153, fat 11.6, fiber 3.9, carbs 7.2, protein 6.1

Conclusion

Food is an essential part of our wellbeing and can be a central part of our day to day life. We all try to improve our dietary habits and, at the same time, make our diet healthier, easier and more able. Following a Keto diet will definitely help you achieve many of your dietary goals, helping you eat better in order to feel better and look better. Using aslow cooker will help you to make a Keto diet even more convenient and easy.

There are many questions about what you can eat during Keto diet and this can be overwhelming. That's why this book will be a wonderful asset to you on your Keto journey- you don't need to worry if every ingredient is Keto friendly, you already know they are! Each meal has been carefully reviewed and follows all Keto guidelines. No sense to come up something new or worrying about random recipes- you have all of these ready to go!

There are many rules to the Keto diet but the most important is to eat less carb and more proteins. It is, of course, also important to find the meals that you like to make dieting more able. With such a wide variety of recipes in this book, you are bound to find many that you love.

This book will help you if you have just started the diet or if you are a long time follower. You will find new and exciting meals all that can be made in a flash thanks to the slow cooker. Remember to eat healthy, follow a diet that is right for you and every dish that you make from this cookbook! Happy cooking!

Recipe Index

ALMOND MILK
Ham Frittata, 9
Vanilla Pancakes, 9
Sausage Frittata, 10
Bacon Omelette, 12
Cheesy Turmeric Eggs, 12
Egg Quiche, 13
Egg Bars, 16
Keto Porridge, 18
Vanilla Pancakes, 22
Breakfast Pie, 25
Chia Seeds Pudding, 27
Kale Frittata, 29
Creamy Chicken Thighs, 34
Prawn Stew, 48
Zucchini Gratin, 52
Moroccan Eggplant Mash, 53
Broccoli Stew, 54
Tomato Gratin with Bell Pepper, 56
Spicy Mushrooms, 56
Vegetable Stew, 57
Layered Mushrooms, 59
Rutabaga Wedges, 59
Creamy Eggplant Salad, 60
Slow Cooker Broccoli Rabe, 61
Soft Keto Kale Salad, 61
Kale Mash with Blue Cheese, 64
Marinated Fennel Bulb, 65
Turkey Meatballs, 66
Parmesan Green Beans, 68
Onion Rings, 71
Tilapia Bites, 75
Crab Dip with Mushrooms, 79
Keto Chocolate Bars, 83
Spoon Cake, 86
Blueberry Pie, 88
Sweet Zucchini Muffins, 89
Chocolate Mousse, 90
Coconut Bars, 90
Vanilla Cream, 91
Dessert Pancakes, 92
Mini Pumpkin Cakes, 95
Walnut Muffins, 96
Vanilla Rolls, 96
Lava Cake, 97
Keto Sweet Bread, 97
Pecan Cookies, 98
Tender Lime Cake, 99

ALMONDS
Soft Keto Kale Salad, 61
Breakfast Turkey Roll, 17
Coconut Kale, 56
Tender Green Cabbage, 58
Almond Cookies, 87
Candied Almonds, 91
Chewy Seed and Nut Bars, 94
Keto Almond Scones, 110

ARTICHOKE
Garlic Artichoke, 54
Artichoke Hummus, 80

ASPARAGUS
Egg Casserole, 11

AVOCADO
Salmon and Avocado Breakfast Bake, 14
Avocado Boats, 24
Avocado Tuna Balls, 28
Pulled Pork Salad, 42
Green Bean and Avocado Salad, 62
Wrapped Avocado Sticks, 66
Avocado Muffins, 87
Avocado Bars, 97

BACON
Bacon Omelette, 12
Keto Egg Muffins, 15
Breakfast Bacon and Eggs, 17
Bacon Beef Casserole, 20
Bacon Pecan Bok Choy, 27
Bacon Meatloaf, 39
Spicy Bacon Strips, 41
Chicken in Bacon, 46
Bacon Wrapped Cauliflower. 51
Sautéed Bell Peppers, 54
Slow Cooker Broccoli Rabe, 61
Soft Keto Kale Salad, 61
Wrapped Avocado Sticks, 66
Wrapped Prawns in Bacon, 67
Crunchy Bacon, 73
Bacon Wrapped Duck Roll, 80
Eggplant Bacon Fries, 81
Bacon Pepper Quiche, 81
Soft Bacon Cookies, 84
Corned Beef, 31
Sweet Bacon Slices, 86
Black Soybeans, 65

BEANS (GREEN)
Cumin Green Beans, 57
Green Bean and Avocado Salad, 62
Parmesan Green Beans, 68

BEEF
Breakfast Ground Beef Casserole, 13
Breakfast Meat Bowl, 16
Bacon Beef Casserole, 20
Moroccan Meatballs, 26
Basil Meatballs, 28
Keto Lasagna, 30
Corned Beef, 31
Beef Curry, 36
Keto Chili, 37
Delicious Turmeric Beef Stew, 40
Seasoned Mini Meatballs, 73
Mushroom Stuffed Meatballs, 81
Bacon Pecan Bok Choy, 27
Balsamic Beef, 36
Keto Beef Ribs, 39
Asian Chopped Beef, 40
Marinated Beef Tenderloin, 45

BELL PEPPER
Slow Cooker Veggie Egg Bake, 11
Keto Chili, 37
Cayenne Pepper Drumsticks, 47
Tomato Gratin with Bell Pepper, 56
Ground Chicken Pepper Meatballs, 72
Ground Pork Bowl, 37
Mushroom Stew, 50
Sautéed Bell Peppers, 54
Creamy Eggplant Salad, 60
Breakfast Sweet Pepper Hash, 23

BELL PEPPER (GREEN)
Egg Bars, 16
Veggie Turkey Smash, 22
Collard Greens, 25
Bacon Pepper Quiche, 81
Garlic Peppers, 58

BELL PEPPER (RED)
Spicy Bacon Strips, 41

BLACKBERRIES
Keto Cobbler, 83

BLUEBERRY
Blueberry Pie, 88

BOK CHOY
Bacon Pecan Bok Choy, 27

BROCCOLI
Broccoli Muffins, 14
Lamb Stew, 40
Delicious Turmeric Beef Stew, 40
Handmade Sausage Stew, 44

Chinese Broccoli, 49
Cauliflower Casserole, 51
Broccoli Balls, 77
Slow Cooker Broccoli Rabe, 61

BRUSSEL SPROUTS
Brussel Sprouts Eggs, 16
Brussel Sprouts with Parmesan, 58
Sweet Brussel Sprouts, 75

BUTTER
Ham Frittata, 9
Sausage Frittata, 10
Slow Cooker Veggie Egg Bake, 11
Bacon Omelette, 12
Cheesy Turmeric Eggs, 12
Cauliflower Hash Brown, 12
Egg Quiche, 13
Breakfast Ground Beef Casserole, 13
Salmon and Avocado Breakfast Bake, 14
Broccoli Muffins, 14
Eggs with Greens, 15
Breakfast Bowl, 15
Keto Egg Muffins, 15
Brussel Sprouts Eggs, 16
Breakfast Meat Bowl, 16
Egg Bars, 16
Breakfast Turkey Roll, 17
Breakfast Bacon and Eggs, 17
Mushroom Omelette, 18
Western Omelette, 18
Slow Cooker Sausages, 19
Coconut Porridge, 19
Salmon Cutlets, 20
Bacon Beef Casserole, 20
Breakfast Tender Chicken Strips, 22
Chicken Muffins, 22
Veggie Turkey Smash, 22
Avocado Boats, 24
Cabbage Rolls, 24
Collard Greens, 25
Breakfast Pie, 25
Moroccan Meatballs, 26
Chia Seeds Pudding, 27
Basil Meatballs, 28
Kale Frittata, 29
Keto Lasagna, 30
Butter Chicken, 30
Corned Beef, 31
Sardine Pate, 32
Spare Ribs, 32
Lamb Chops, 33
Rabbit Stew, 34
Duck Breast, 35
Jerk Chicken, 35

Beef Curry, 36
Keto Chili, 37
Ground Pork Bowl, 37
Marinated Greek Style Pork, 38
Shredded Chicken, 38
Bacon Meatloaf, 39
Keto Pork Tenderloin, 39
Spicy Bacon Strips, 41
Chicken Stew, 41
Garlic Pork Belly, 42
Sesame Seed Shrimp, 42
Cod Fillet in Coconut Flakes, 43
Chicken Liver Pate, 43
Garlic Duck Breast, 43
Handmade Sausage Stew, 44
Marinated Beef Tenderloin, 45
Chicken Liver Sauté, 45
Chicken in Bacon, 46
Whole Chicken, 46
Cayenne Pepper Drumsticks, 47
Prawn Stew, 48
Pork-Jalapeno Bowl, 48
Chicken Marsala, 48
Zucchini Pasta, 49
Slow Cooker Spaghetti Squash, 49
Mushroom Stew, 50
Cabbage Steaks, 50
Mashed Cauliflower, 50
Bacon Wrapped Cauliflower. 51
Cauliflower Casserole, 51
Cauliflower Rice, 51
Curry Cauliflower, 52
Garlic Cauliflower Steaks, 52
Zucchini Gratin, 52
Eggplant Gratin, 53
Moroccan Eggplant Mash, 53
Sautéed Bell Peppers, 54
Garlic Artichoke, 54
Broccoli Stew, 54
Spiced Fennel Slices, 55
Okra Stew, 55
Sesame Snow Peas, 55
Coconut Kale, 56
Tomato Gratin with Bell Pepper, 56
Cumin Green Beans, 57
Vegetable Stew, 57
Garlic Peppers, 58
Tender Green Cabbage, 58
Layered Mushrooms, 59
Rutabaga Wedges, 59
Thai Cabbage, 60
Eggplant Hash, 60
Slow Cooker Broccoli Rabe, 61
Keto Leeks, 61
Green Bean and Avocado Salad, 62

Cauliflower Puree with Parmesan, 62
Cauliflower Croquettes, 63
Cheesy Spaghetti Squash, 63
Pesto Spaghetti Squash, 64
Zucchini Slices with Mozzarella, 64
Kale Mash with Blue Cheese, 64
Black Soybeans, 65
Marinated Fennel Bulb, 65
Pumpkin Cubes, 65
Wrapped Avocado Sticks, 66
Deviled Eggs, 66
Chicken and Cauliflower Pizza, 67
Cauliflower Bites, 67
Wrapped Prawns in Bacon, 67
Buffalo Chicken Wings, 68
Eggplant Fries, 68
Zucchini Fries, 69
Cauliflower Fritters, 69
Zucchini Latkes, 69
Zucchini Tots with Cheese, 70
Spicy & Salty Keto Nuts, 70
Jalapeno Fritters, 70
Onion Rings, 71
Sweet and Spicy Chicken Wings, 71
Ground Chicken Pepper Meatballs, 72
Pork Nuggets, 72
Pulled Pork, 73
Crunchy Bacon, 73
Mini Chicken Meatballs, 74
Spinach Rolls, 74
Pork Belly Bites, 74
Mushroom Skewers, 75
Stuffed Mushrooms, 76
Caprese Meatballs, 76
Broccoli Balls, 77
White Queso Dip, 78
Keto Crackers, 79
Chia Crackers, 79
Artichoke Hummus, 80
Bacon Wrapped Duck Roll, 80
Mini Muffins, 82
Eggplant Rolls with Meat, 82
Keto Cobbler, 83
Soft Bacon Cookies, 84
Keto Brownies, 84
Keto Peanut Butter Cookies, 84
Keto Chip Cookies, 85
Coconut Bars, 85
Spoon Cake, 86
Sweet Bacon Slices, 86
Pound Cake, 86
Sweet Sesame Buns, 87
Almond Cookies, 87
Avocado Muffins, 87
Walnut Balls, 88

Rhubarb Crumble, 88
Blueberry Pie, 88
Sesame Cookies, 89
Keto Soufflé, 89
Sweet Zucchini Muffins, 89
Keto Truffles, 90
Coconut Bars, 90
Snowball Cookies, 91
Dessert Pancakes, 92
Pudding Cake, 92
Keto Fudge, 93
Gingerbread Cookies, 93
Chewy Seed and Nut Bars, 94
Red Velvet Cupcakes, 94
Keto Cheesecake, 94
Lavender Cookies, 95
Mini Pumpkin Cakes, 95
Walnut Muffins, 96
Vanilla Rolls, 96
Cinnamon Swirls, 96
Keto Sweet Bread, 97
Avocado Bars, 97
Raspberry Tart, 98
Rhubarb Bars, 98
Flax Seeds Balls, 99
Sunflower Seeds Cookies, 99

CABBAGE
Cabbage Rolls, 24
Broccoli Stew, 54
Tender Green Cabbage, 58

CABBAGE (GREEN)
Tender Green Cabbage, 58

CABBAGE (RED)
Red Cabbage Slices, 62

CABBAGE (WHITE)
Cabbage Steaks, 50
Vegetable Stew, 57
Thai Cabbage, 60

CAULIFLOWER
Slow Cooker Veggie Egg Bake, 11
Cauliflower Hash Brown, 12
Egg Quiche, 13
Breakfast Pie, 25
Chicken Stew, 41
Mashed Cauliflower, 50
Cauliflower Rice, 51
Curry Cauliflower, 52
Sautéed Bell Peppers, 54
Okra Stew, 55
Vegetable Stew, 57

Cauliflower Puree with Parmesan, 62
Cauliflower Croquettes, 63
Chicken and Cauliflower Pizza, 67
Cauliflower Fritters, 69
Cauliflower Bread, 80
Bacon Wrapped Cauliflower. 51
Cauliflower Casserole, 51
Garlic Cauliflower Steaks, 52
Cauliflower Bites, 67

CELERY
Slow Cooker Veggie Egg Bake, 11
Breakfast Turkey Roll, 17
Whole Chicken, 46

CHEESE (BLUE)
Kale Mash with Blue Cheese, 64

CHEESE (CHEDDAR)
Breakfast Sweet Pepper Hash, 23
White Queso Dip, 78
Crab Dip with Mushrooms, 79

CHEESE (MONTEREY JACK)
White Queso Dip, 78

CHEESE (MOZZARELLA)
Zucchini Slices with Mozzarella, 64
Meat Balls with Mozzarella, 72
Eggplant Rolls with Meat, 82

CHEESE (PARMESAN)
Sausage Frittata, 10
Breakfast Meat Casserole, 10
Egg Casserole, 11
Cheesy Turmeric Eggs, 12
Cauliflower Hash Brown, 12
Keto Egg Muffins, 15
Western Omelette, 18
Breakfast Pizza, 22
Breakfast Pie, 25
Keto Lasagna, 30
Tuscan Chicken, 31
Prawn Stew, 48
Zucchini Gratin, 52
Eggplant Gratin, 53
Tomato Gratin with Bell Pepper, 56
Brussel Sprouts with Parmesan, 58
Slow Cooker Broccoli Rabe, 61
Cauliflower Puree with Parmesan, 62
Cheesy Spaghetti Squash, 63
Parmesan Green Beans, 68
Zucchini Tots with Cheese, 70
Keto Tortillas with Cheese, 71
Sweet Brussel Sprouts, 75

Broccoli Balls, 77
Keto Bread Sticks, 78
Cheesy Zucchini Crisps, 78
Mushroom Stuffed Meatballs, 81
Bacon Pepper Quiche, 81
Grated Zucchini with Cheese, 63

CHIA SEEDS
Chia Seeds Pudding, 27
Chia Crackers, 79

CHICKEN
Breakfast Meat Casserole, 10
Breakfast Meat Bowl, 16
Slow Cooker Sausages, 19
Chicken Muffins, 22
Breakfast Pie, 25
Bacon Meatloaf, 39
Whole Chicken, 46
Chicken and Cauliflower Pizza, 67
Ground Chicken Pepper Meatballs, 72
Mini Chicken Meatballs, 74
Spinach Rolls, 74
Breakfast Bowl, 15
Breakfast Tender Chicken Strips, 22
Paprika Shrimp, 22
Breakfast Sweet Pepper Hash, 23
Chicken Bites, 23
Cabbage Rolls, 24
Collard Greens, 25
Moroccan Meatballs, 26
Breakfast Shredded Pork, 27
Prosciutto Chicken Nuggets, 28
Butter Chicken, 30
Tuscan Chicken, 31
Creamy Chicken Thighs, 34
Jerk Chicken, 35
Shredded Chicken, 38
Chicken Stew, 41
Chicken Liver Pate, 43
Chicken Liver Sauté, 45
Chicken in Bacon, 46
Keto Adobo Chicken, 47
Cayenne Pepper Drumsticks, 47
Keto BBQ Chicken Wings, 47
Chicken Marsala, 48
Curry Cauliflower, 52
Buffalo Chicken Wings, 68
Sweet and Spicy Chicken Wings, 71
Chicken Tenders, 77
Garlic Chicken Wings, 77
Eggplant Rolls with Meat, 82

CHILI FLAKES
Breakfast Ground Beef Casserole, 13

Eggs with Greens, 15
Breakfast Bowl, 15
Egg Bars, 16
Breakfast Turkey Roll, 17
Mushroom Omelette, 18
Slow Cooker Sausages, 19
Chicken Muffins, 22
Veggie Turkey Smash, 22
Breakfast Sweet Pepper Hash, 23
Pork Breakfast Sausages, 23
Prosciutto Chicken Nuggets, 28
Keto Lasagna, 30
Tuscan Chicken, 31
Corned Beef, 31
Pork Shoulder, 32
Chili Verde, 38
Pulled Pork Salad, 42
Garlic Duck Breast, 43
Chicken in Bacon, 46
Prawn Stew, 48
Pork-Jalapeno Bowl, 48
Chinese Broccoli, 49
Cabbage Steaks, 50
Cauliflower Casserole, 51
Eggplant Gratin, 53
Spicy Mushrooms, 56
Vegetable Stew, 57
Slow Cooker Broccoli Rabe, 61
Black Soybeans, 65
Keto Tortillas with Cheese, 71
Sweet and Spicy Chicken Wings, 71
Meat Balls with Mozzarella, 72
Cheesy Zucchini Crisps, 78
Cauliflower Bread, 80

CHOCOLATE
Keto Brownies, 84
Chocolate Mousse, 90
Keto Truffles, 90
Pudding Cake, 92
Keto Fudge, 93
Lava Cake, 97
Keto Chocolate Bars, 83
Spoon Cake, 86
Keto Soufflé, 89

COCONUT CREAM
Coconut Porridge, 19

COCONUT FLAKES
Avocado Tuna Balls, 28
Basil Meatballs, 28
Cod Fillet in Coconut Flakes, 43
Coconut Kale, 56
Zucchini Slices with Mozzarella, 64

Onion Rings, 71
Sweet and Spicy Chicken Wings, 71
Meat Balls with Mozzarella, 72
Keto Peanut Butter Cookies, 84
Coconut Bars, 85
Sweet Sesame Buns, 87
Coconut Bars, 90
Snowball Cookies, 91
Chewy Seed and Nut Bars, 94
Flax Seeds Balls, 99

COCONUT MILK
Sautéed Bell Peppers, 54
Coconut Kale, 56
Cumin Green Beans, 57
Creamy Eggplant Salad, 60
Keto Almond Scones, 110

COCONUT OIL
Thai Cabbage, 60

COD
Cod Bites, 26
Cod Fillet in Coconut Flakes, 43

COLLARD GREENS
Collard Greens, 25

CRAB
Crab Dip with Mushrooms, 79

CREAM CHEESE
Breakfast Bowl, 15
Creamy Chicken Thighs, 34
Keto Leeks, 61
Keto Bread Sticks, 78
Pound Cake, 86
Chocolate Mousse, 90
Keto Fudge, 93
Keto Cheesecake, 94

CUCUMBER
Soft Keto Kale Salad, 61
Green Bean and Avocado Salad, 62

CURRY PASTE
Beef Curry, 36
Curry Cauliflower, 52
Thai Cabbage, 60
Asian Pork with Keto Tortillas, 76

DUCK
Duck Breast, 35
Garlic Duck Breast, 43
Duck Rolls, 46

Bacon Wrapped Duck Roll, 80

EGGPLANT
Veggie Turkey Smash, 22
Lamb Stew, 40
Autumn Pork Stew, 44
Moroccan Eggplant Mash, 53
Layered Mushrooms, 59
Creamy Eggplant Salad, 60
Eggplant Fries, 68
Mushroom Skewers, 75
Rabbit Stew, 34
Mushroom Stew, 50
Eggplant Gratin, 53
Eggplant Hash, 60
Eggplant Bacon Fries, 81
Eggplant Rolls with Meat, 82

EGGS
Ham Frittata, 9
Vanilla Pancakes, 9
Sausage Frittata, 10
Egg Casserole, 11
Slow Cooker Veggie Egg Bake, 11
Bacon Omelette, 12
Cheesy Turmeric Eggs, 12
Cauliflower Hash Brown, 12
Egg Quiche, 13
Salmon and Avocado Breakfast Bake, 14
Broccoli Muffins, 14
Eggs with Greens, 15
Breakfast Bowl, 15
Keto Egg Muffins, 15
Brussel Sprouts Eggs, 16
Egg Bars, 16
Breakfast Bacon and Eggs, 17
Mushroom Omelette, 18
Western Omelette, 18
Slow Cooker Sausages, 19
Coconut Porridge, 19
Chicken Muffins, 22
Vanilla Pancakes, 22
Breakfast Pizza, 22
Chicken Bites, 23
Avocado Boats, 24
Breakfast Pie, 25
Cod Bites, 26
Moroccan Meatballs, 26
Avocado Tuna Balls, 28
Basil Meatballs, 28
Kale Frittata, 29
Bacon Meatloaf, 39
Paprika Pork Sausages, 41
Cod Fillet in Coconut Flakes, 43
Handmade Sausage Stew, 44

Cauliflower Croquettes, 63
Deviled Eggs, 66
Chicken and Cauliflower Pizza, 67
Cauliflower Bites, 67
Zucchini Fries, 69
Cauliflower Fritters, 69
Zucchini Tots with Cheese, 70
Jalapeno Fritters, 70
Onion Rings, 71
Keto Tortillas with Cheese, 71
Ground Chicken Pepper Meatballs, 72
Pork Nuggets, 72
Seasoned Mini Meatballs, 73
Mini Chicken Meatballs, 74
Caprese Meatballs, 76
Chicken Tenders, 77
Broccoli Balls, 77
Keto Bread Sticks, 78
Chia Crackers, 79
Cauliflower Bread, 80
Bacon Pepper Quiche, 81
Mini Muffins, 82
Keto Chocolate Bars, 83
Keto Cobbler, 83
Soft Bacon Cookies, 84
Keto Brownies, 84
Mint Pudding, 85
Keto Chip Cookies, 85
Coconut Bars, 85
Pound Cake, 86
Sweet Sesame Buns, 87
Avocado Muffins, 87
Walnut Balls, 88
Sesame Cookies, 89
Keto Soufflé, 89
Chocolate Mousse, 90
Keto Truffles, 90
Vanilla Cream, 91
Snowball Cookies, 91
Dessert Pancakes, 92
Cinnamon Cup Cake, 92
Pudding Cake, 92
Kombucha Cake, 93
Gingerbread Cookies, 93
Red Velvet Cupcakes, 94
Keto Cheesecake, 94
Lavender Cookies, 95
Walnut Muffins, 96
Keto Almond Scones, 110

ERYTHRITOL
Jerk Chicken, 35
Mint Pudding, 85
Keto Chip Cookies, 85
Spoon Cake, 86

Sweet Bacon Slices, 86
Sweet Sesame Buns, 87
Almond Cookies, 87
Walnut Balls, 88
Rhubarb Crumble, 88
Blueberry Pie, 88
Keto Soufflé, 89
Sweet Zucchini Muffins, 89
Keto Truffles, 90
Vanilla Cream, 91
Snowball Cookies, 91
Pudding Cake, 92
Keto Fudge, 93
Kombucha Cake, 93
Chewy Seed and Nut Bars, 94
Red Velvet Cupcakes, 94
Keto Cheesecake, 94
Vanilla Rolls, 96
Cinnamon Swirls, 96
Keto Sweet Bread, 97
Raspberry Tart, 98
Pecan Cookies, 98
Tender Lime Cake, 99

FENNEL
Spiced Fennel Slices, 55
Marinated Fennel Bulb, 65

FLAKES
Rabbit Stew, 34

FULL-FAT CREAM
Breakfast Shredded Pork, 27
Tuscan Chicken, 31
Marinated Greek Style Pork, 38
Mashed Cauliflower, 50
White Queso Dip, 78
Mint Pudding, 85
Pudding Cake, 92

GHEE
Bacon Beef Casserole, 20
Vanilla Pancakes, 22
Breakfast Sweet Pepper Hash, 23
Pork Breakfast Sausages, 23
Cod Bites, 26
Prosciutto Chicken Nuggets, 28

HAM
Ham Frittata, 9
Western Omelette, 18
Breakfast Pizza, 22

HAZELNUTS
Spicy & Salty Keto Nuts, 70

HEAVY CREAM
Western Omelette, 18
Keto Lasagna, 30

KALE
Kale Frittata, 29
Coconut Kale, 56
Soft Keto Kale Salad, 61
Kale Mash with Blue Cheese, 64

LAMB
Rosemary Leg of Lamb, 33
Lamb Chops, 33
Thyme Lamb Chops, 44

LEEK
Keto Leeks, 61

LETTUCE
Pulled Pork Salad, 42

LIME
Tender Lime Cake, 99

MARSALA
Chicken Marsala, 48

MUSHROOMS
Breakfast Ground Beef Casserole, 13
Mushroom Omelette, 18
Cabbage Rolls, 24
Spicy Mushrooms, 56
Stuffed Mushrooms, 76

MUSHROOMS (WHITE)
Autumn Pork Stew, 44
Chicken Liver Sauté, 45
Chicken Marsala, 48
Mushroom Stew, 50
Cauliflower Casserole, 51
Vegetable Stew, 57
Layered Mushrooms, 59
Eggplant Hash, 60
Mushroom Skewers, 75
Crab Dip with Mushrooms, 79
Mushroom Stuffed Meatballs, 81

MUSTARD
Asian Chopped Beef, 40
Garlic Pork Belly, 42
Keto BBQ Chicken Wings, 47
Corned Beef, 31
Rosemary Leg of Lamb, 33

NUTMEG
Vanilla Pancakes, 22
Peppered Steak, 34
Jerk Chicken, 35
Shredded Chicken, 38
Chicken Liver Pate, 43
Marinated Beef Tenderloin, 45
Slow Cooker Spaghetti Squash, 49
Moroccan Eggplant Mash, 53
Garlic Peppers, 58
Eggplant Bacon Fries, 81

OKRA
Okra Stew, 55

ONION
Breakfast Meat Casserole, 10
Breakfast Bacon and Eggs, 17
Mushroom Omelette, 18
Salmon Cutlets, 20
Bacon Beef Casserole, 20
Veggie Turkey Smash, 22
Breakfast Sweet Pepper Hash, 23
Pork Breakfast Sausages, 23
Collard Greens, 25
Breakfast Pie, 25
Pork Shoulder, 32
Rosemary Leg of Lamb, 33
Creamy Chicken Thighs, 34
Rabbit Stew, 34
Beef Curry, 36
Keto Chili, 37
Ground Pork Bowl, 37
Keto Beef Ribs, 39
Lamb Stew, 40
Delicious Turmeric Beef Stew, 40
Spicy Bacon Strips, 41
Paprika Pork Sausages, 41
Chicken Stew, 41
Chicken Liver Pate, 43
Thyme Lamb Chops, 44
Chicken Liver Sauté, 45
Whole Chicken, 46
Pork-Jalapeno Bowl, 48
Mushroom Stew, 50
Sautéed Bell Peppers, 54
Okra Stew, 55
Spicy Mushrooms, 56
Layered Mushrooms, 59
Eggplant Hash, 60
Zucchini Latkes, 69
Onion Rings, 71
Mini Chicken Meatballs, 74

ONION (WHITE)
Autumn Pork Stew, 44

PEAS
Sesame Snow Peas, 55

PECANS
Bacon Pecan Bok Choy, 27
Pecan Cookies, 98

PEPPER (CHILI)
Duck Breast, 35
Keto Beef Ribs, 39
Bacon Meatloaf, 39
Cayenne Pepper Drumsticks, 47
Deviled Eggs, 66
Cauliflower Bites, 67

PEPPER (JALAPENO)
Moroccan Eggplant Mash, 53
Creamy Eggplant Salad, 60
White Queso Dip, 78
Pork-Jalapeno Bowl, 48
Jalapeno Fritters, 70

PEPPER CHILI (GREEN)
Chili Verde, 38

PORK
Breakfast Meat Casserole, 10
Breakfast Sweet Pepper Hash, 23
Pork Breakfast Sausages, 23
Ground Pork Bowl, 37
Paprika Pork Sausages, 41
Handmade Sausage Stew, 44
Meat Balls with Mozzarella, 72
Breakfast Shredded Pork, 27
Spare Ribs, 32
Pork Shoulder, 32
Chili Verde, 38
Marinated Greek Style Pork, 38
Keto Pork Tenderloin, 39
Pulled Pork Salad, 42
Garlic Pork Belly, 42
Autumn Pork Stew, 44
Pork-Jalapeno Bowl, 48
Pork Nuggets, 72
Pulled Pork, 73
Pork Belly Bites, 74
Asian Pork with Keto Tortillas, 76

PRAWNS
Prawn Stew, 48
Wrapped Prawns in Bacon, 67

PROSCIUTTO
Prosciutto Chicken Nuggets, 28

PUMPKIN
Pumpkin Cubes, 65
Mini Pumpkin Cakes, 95
Pesto Spaghetti Squash, 64
Spicy & Salty Keto Nuts, 70
Chewy Seed and Nut Bars, 94
Keto Sweet Bread, 97

RASPBERRIES
Raspberry Tart, 98

RHUBARB
Rhubarb Crumble, 88
Rhubarb Bars, 98

RUTABAGA
Curled Rutabaga, 59
Rutabaga Wedges, 59

SALMON
Salmon and Avocado Breakfast Bake, 14
Salmon Cutlets, 20
Sardine Pate, 32

SAUCE (HOT)
Buffalo Chicken Wings, 68
Mini Chicken Meatballs, 74

SAUSAGES
Sausage Frittata, 10

SHRIMP
Paprika Shrimp, 22
Sesame Seed Shrimp, 42

SIRLOIN
Peppered Steak, 34

SPAGHETTI
Slow Cooker Spaghetti Squash, 49
Cheesy Spaghetti Squash, 63
Pesto Spaghetti Squash, 64

SPINACH
Butter Chicken, 30
Tuscan Chicken, 31
Keto Chili, 37
Duck Rolls, 46
Broccoli Stew, 54
Vegetable Stew, 57
Pesto Spaghetti Squash, 64
Seasoned Mini Meatballs, 73

Stuffed Mushrooms, 76
Spinach Rolls, 74

STEVIA
Keto Porridge, 18
Duck Breast, 35
Keto BBQ Chicken Wings, 47
Pumpkin Cubes, 65
Crunchy Bacon, 73
Mini Chicken Meatballs, 74
Keto Chocolate Bars, 83
Keto Cobbler, 83
Keto Brownies, 84
Keto Peanut Butter Cookies, 84
Avocado Muffins, 87
Walnut Balls, 88
Keto Cheesecake, 94
Walnut Muffins, 96
Lava Cake, 97
Avocado Bars, 97
Rhubarb Bars, 98
Flax Seeds Balls, 99
Sunflower Seeds Cookies, 99
Vanilla Pancakes, 8
Coconut Porridge, 19
Chia Seeds Pudding, 27
Soft Bacon Cookies, 84
Cinnamon Cup Cake, 92

SWERVE
Chewy Seed and Nut Bars, 94

TILAPIA
Tilapia Bites, 75

TOMATO PASTE
Keto BBQ Chicken Wings, 47

TOMATOES
Egg Casserole, 11
Egg Quiche, 13
Keto Beef Ribs, 39
Chicken Stew, 41
Pulled Pork Salad, 42
Handmade Sausage Stew, 44
Breakfast Meat Bowl, 16
Bacon Beef Casserole, 20
Keto Lasagna, 30
Lamb Chops, 33
Keto Chili, 37
Pulled Pork, 73

Cauliflower Casserole, 51
Tomato Gratin with Bell Pepper, 56
Caprese Meatballs, 76

TORTILLAS
Asian Pork with Keto Tortillas, 76

TUNA
Avocado Tuna Balls, 28

TURKEY
Veggie Turkey Smash, 22
Turkey Meatballs, 66
Caprese Meatballs, 76
Breakfast Turkey Roll, 17

ULL-FAT CREAM
Keto Brownies, 84

WALNUTS
Green Bean and Avocado Salad, 62
Spicy & Salty Keto Nuts, 70
Walnut Balls, 88
Rhubarb Crumble, 88
Cinnamon Cup Cake, 92
Mini Pumpkin Cakes, 95
Walnut Muffins, 96

WHIPPED CREAM
Mint Pudding, 85
Keto Soufflé, 89
Red Velvet Cupcakes, 94

ZUCCHINI
Breakfast Ground Beef Casserole, 13
Rabbit Stew, 34
Lamb Stew, 40
Chicken Stew, 41
Zucchini Pasta, 49
Zucchini Gratin, 52
Zucchini Fettuccine, 57
Grated Zucchini with Cheese, 63
Zucchini Slices with Mozzarella, 64
Zucchini Fries, 69
Zucchini Latkes, 69
Zucchini Tots with Cheese, 70
Cheesy Zucchini Crisps, 78
Sweet Zucchini Muffins, 89

CPSIA information can be obtained
at www.ICGtesting.com
Printed in the USA
BVHW051700100723
667017BV00006B/268